PARENTING
WITH PIECES

PARENTING as a CATALYST for
PERSONAL GROWTH

CALVIN
WITCHER

CANEWOOD
an imprint of Witcher Publishing Group

Parenting with Pieces. Copyright © 2016 by Calvin Witcher

Published and distributed by Canewood, an imprint of Witcher Publishing Group.

Cover Design: Calvin Witcher
Interior Design: Calvin Witcher

This book may be purchased in bulk for educational, business, fundraising, or sales promotional use. For Information, please email info@witcherpublishing.com

Publishing consultation, support, design, and composition by Witcher Publishing Group. **www.witcherpublishing.com.**

Library of Congress Cataloging-in-Publication Data

Library of Congress Control Number: 2015920907
Trade Paperback ISBN: 978-0-9971151-1-6
Trade Hardcover ISBN: 978-0-9971151-2-3
E-Book ISBN: 978-0-9971151-0-9

Witcher Publishing Group - rev. date: 01/04/2016

Witcher &o Canewood
Visit CanewoodBooks.com

Words of Praise For *Parenting With Pieces* and Calvin Witcher

"My friend Calvin Witcher writes brilliantly and succinctly in *Parenting with Pieces*. This book is based somewhat on his own personal, puzzled, and powerful experience as a parent, and through this book you see an evolving person enjoying his personal unfolding of Self and expanded consciousness."

— DR. CARLTON D. PEARSON
International Teacher, Stellar Award winning vocalist, and
Author of *The Gospel of Inclusion* and
God Is Not A Christian, Nor A Jew, Muslim, Hindu …
God Dwells With Us, In Us, Around Us, As Us

"Calvin Witcher isn't lying when he tells you *Parenting with Pieces* isn't just for parents! I started this book expecting to find helpful ways to deal with my children when they misbehave, or better yet, specific ways on how to prevent them from misbehaving in the first place. Instead, I was delighted to find this book is everything Mr. Witcher promises in his preface and specifically "a guide to manipulate your life in your favor." He's not lying when he says that!

Mr. Witcher uses real life examples with his husband and children to explain the ways he came to understand how we should divide our life into pieces and then how to fit those pieces together to guide our thoughts and actions. Whether you're a parent of children or not, you can use these insights into his life to rearrange your perspective, recognize your genius, claim your identity, minimize and cope with your stress, and have a better understanding of your emotions. Combining these pieces improves not only your parenting (children or otherwise) but also influences your life in the direction you want it to go.

Parenting with Pieces will teach you or remind you to take care of yourself first, to reflect on where your life is now and where you want it to be, and shows that changing the way we think can drastically improve not only our outlook on life but also how well we function daily."

— SHELL TAYLOR
Dreamspinner Press Author of *Redeeming Hope*
(Book #1 of *Home for Hope*)

"A must-read, DEFINITIVE guide that will totally redefine how you see yourself personally AND as a parent. Calvin's ability to relate to parent's real internal battles is the premise of why this book is not only effective but a game changer. I can only imagine how different the world would have been if this book was only written 50 years ago. GENIUS!!"

— BENNIE MAYBERRY
Social Advocate, Marketing Guru, and
Founder of Positive Minded People

"Calvin has been a go-to resource for me on many subjects but primarily parenting. His vast knowledge on how to manage yourself as a new parent has been invaluable to our new family. This book will frequently be referenced for years to come."

— AMY MUCKEN
Culture Expert at
A Courageous Creative Culture
accculture.com

"Calvin Witcher is a most diligent, energetic, and well-informed person with regard to parenting issues. He is one of the few people who understands and can write about the real needs of families. Moreover, he can do this in an engaging fashion that does not put parents off. For the sake of families everywhere, I hope that his book is widely read and taken to heart."

— J. THOMAS, M.DIV, PH.D

"Calvin is a one-of-a-kind person. He is fun, energetic, and extremely wise. He is beyond his years in knowledge and skill. I feel fortunate to know him and work side-by-side with him."

— ALLISON CHERRY, LCSW
Los Angeles County
Department of Children and Family Services

"*Parenting with Pieces* is one of the most intelligently affirming books I've read … Calvin's book encouraged me that, together with the help of my spouse and community, I *can* do this."

— JONATHAN HANNEMAN

"I've known Calvin for several years now … His knowledge, teachings, and values are excellent. He truly lives what he teaches."

— PETE
Los Angeles, CA

Words of Praise

"Calvin Witcher is a mastermind when it comes to helping individuals and families. I have co-trained with him for the last 3 years, and he is fabulous. He is so full of wisdom and humor. The individual that reads this book will be fortunate to get a taste of what people in Southern California know—Calvin is incredible!!!!"

— LORI SWITANOWSKI, LMFT
Director of Our Family Comes First

"I have known Mr. Witcher for many years. I am familiar with him personally and professionally. In every setting, Calvin remains consistent, professional, kind, and it is a joy to be in his presence. His gift to teach and train is unparalleled, and the integrity and passion he brings to the table is matchless. His insights on personal progress and parenting are beyond theory—I have firsthand experience that it works! I have had numerous occasions to observe him in his family setting. His ability to relate with his children is truly awesome—he sets the bar for parenting."

— DR. BEAU STOCKING

"Calvin has always presented in a professional manner while working closely with families. He also exhibits a high degree of integrity, judgment, and responsibility. Additionally, he utilizes logical and practical approaches to solve problems when necessary. Calvin is organized, efficient, and willing to go above and beyond parent training ..."

— JUAN F. ALVAREZ, MPA
Foster/Kinship Program Director
Los Angeles City College

"Calvin is very knowledgeable especially in the field of foster and adoptive care. He is approachable, professional, and his teaching skills are superb."

— LIL E. SASS, MA
Foster/Kinship Program Coordinator

"Calvin tells it like it is. He doesn't sugar coat but rather gives you all the possible scenarios. In doing so, he pushes you to question your preconceptions and embrace your strengths and challenges while instilling a desire to continue to learn and grow."

— SARAH AND BEN MALONEY
Graduate of Calvin's Training for Parents

PARENTING WITH PIECES

"I have worked with Calvin Witcher as a co-trainer in the pre-licensing classes for foster and adoptive parents for several years. He is an energetic and passionate person who cares deeply for the children from abused backgrounds and the families who care for them."

— KAREN DIXON, MS
Foster/Kinship Program Coordinator
San Bernardino Valley College

"If you are looking for a teacher who embodies the love, passion, and knowledge ... Calvin Witcher is the perfect candidate. I am consistently referring back to my many notes taken to assist me in my daily parenting. ... be prepared to have a thoroughly enjoyable learning experience with many 'aha' moments."

— BYRAN HARDING
Graduate of Calvin's Training for Parents

"Calvin Witcher's teachings are profound, timeless, and life changing. He knows how to share his heart and home with his friends and family in a very loving, supportive way. He is my 'Soul' brotha from another mother."

— fiZ
Author of *Ignite the Rock-Star Within*

"He is a man who truly cares for one's well being and only wants the best for people."

— MARK AND ANNA CHRISTI KHACHATOORIAN
Graduate of Calvin's Training for Parents

Table of Contents

Dedication

Parenting with Pieces is dedicated to
Jeremy James Witcher,
who has supported me through
every transition of our life together,
and without whom none of this
would have been possible.

And to my wonderful sons,
Daniel, Kendrick, Brian, and Dante,
who helped inspire this book.

I love you all more
than words can express.

Thank you for being the
best family in the world.

.

Foreword

A puzzle is designed to cause feelings of confusion, intrigue, and curiosity because it is difficult to understand or make sense of. Puzzles themselves involve and necessitate thinking hard about something difficult to grasp or explain. Life—as most of us know and experience it—is just that, a huge, dramatic, and ongoing puzzle. When you have an inner image or picture of what you perceive as the end result, its a little easier to figure out. Most of it, is learning as you live, or as scripture says—working and walking out your own personal salvation.

Parenting is something I've done—going on twenty-two years—raising my twenty-one-year-old son and eighteen-year-old daughter. Through my sixty-two-year journey of life, I've also spawned and continue to sponsor many non-biological offspring through my ministry, books, award winning gospel recordings, and any number of other results of my virile soul. As Calvin states in his book, the English word 'parent' originates from a Latin and French word that means to "bring forth" or sponsor. We all do that biologically, as foster parents, or as adoptive parents. Parenting is by far the most pronounced, honorable, and sometimes ornery experience in life. In normal cases it involves birthing, (spawning) nurturing, and raising offspring. But, you could parent a person, an idea, a business, ministry, or organization. A fertile life produces and reproduces, generally after its own kind.

PARENTING WITH PIECES

It is said that we are not just human beings looking for spiritual experiences; we are a spirit having an earthly encounter. The basic and most profound lessons of life and spirit come from living life as a spirit through which we experience and express our recovered divinity in the process.

My friend Calvin Witcher writes brilliantly and succinctly in *Parenting with Pieces*. This book is based somewhat on his own personal, puzzled, and powerful experience as a parent, and through this book you see an evolving person enjoying his personal unfolding of Self and expanded consciousness.

Thoughts are powerful. They are both creative and inventive. What we think about—we bring about. The literary journey Calvin takes you on in this book reveals the amazing landscape of human experience. You will see varying levels of unveiling and revealing of powerful inner evolutions and resolutions that are practical and important to each reader individually. Your experience with this book will add to the collective consciousness of all of us who continue to awaken to our higher selves and souls.

Enjoy the ride and don't miss the beautiful scenery.

— **DR. CARLTON D. PEARSON**
International Teacher, Stellar Award winning vocalist, and
Author of *The Gospel of Inclusion* and
God Is Not A Christian, Nor A Jew, Muslim, Hindu …
God Dwells With Us, In Us, Around Us, As Us

Preface

ஓ

How To Use This Book

This book is a roadmap to break free from cultural expectations of a "good parent" providing a framework for personal, empowerment, and freedom. This book will dynamically and drastically change your life. Are you up for the challenge? I know you are, and I am here to partner with you in your journey.

First, let me express my sincere thanks and appreciation to you for reading this book. Whether you bought it, were given the book as a gift, or you are simply perusing the first couple of pages in order to convince yourself to purchase the book—I am grateful. Let me help you out; BUY THE BOOK! Buy this book for yourself and then buy another copy for someone else.

Everything has a beginning, and every beginning has a foundation. My hope is that you will use this book to create or build upon the foundation you already have. Since everything has a foundation, parenting is no exception. Parenting is more than taking care of children. You are a parent **before** you have children not **because** you have children. Parenting, in its simplicity, is about knowing who you are in relation to others. You can be a parent in many different ways. The original meaning of the word parent[1] simply meant to bring forth, give birth to, or produce. Having children is only one faction within the larger community of parenthood.

Yes, individuals that have children are parents but so are many other people. Doctors are parents; they "bring forth" knowledge that helps us continue living healthy lives. They help parents "give birth to" their children and they help "produce" health and hope for us all. Teachers are parents; they "bring forth" information that helps us navigate life more effectively. They "give birth to" the next generation of thinkers and teachers, and what they "produce" is experienced in every form of living especially personally, professionally, politically, and philosophically.

This book is about parenting your soul and cultivating the source of everything that flows from you, to you, and as you— first. We will do this in the context of parenthood, but **this book is more about You** than it is about your child. You need not even have a child for this book to be of benefit to you. Because this book is about you first, it is really about parenting your Self. This book is essentially a guide on how to manipulate life in your favor. Yes, I said manipulate. Many of us have been taught that manipulation is bad and have been programmed to think it should be avoided at all costs. The truth is—we all manipulate. We manipulate for maliciousness or for greatness. I am here to help you do the latter.

We put so much pressure on parents to perform, we often neglect to remember that parents need refueling. This book is more than a tool to help you **perform** better. I want you to

become better. However, your progress is up to you. What you get out of this book will be equivalent to the work you put into this book. I believe you will receive exactly what you are seeking AND receive tools you do not even know you are seeking.

Most parents have an image of what they want in their mind, for their lives, and their family, but have lacked the tools and framework to make it work in real life—*until now. Parenting with Pieces* outlines a path that will make you more confident by meeting your needs first. You'll discover a framework that will accelerate your personal growth and radically improve your effectiveness as a parent.

This book is designed to walk you through your current circumstances. You will find a section at the end of each chapter entitled "Placing The Pieces." Think of this as your personal journal. Use the question and answer format to explore who you are, where you are, and what you want to create. Translate the principles in this book according to your unique situation. I believe you will experience countless benefits if you allow this book to adapt to your specific needs.

Next, I want to thank you for witnessing my personal journey through these pages. I also want to thank you for beginning the process of "waking up" in order to witness, first-hand, your own change, growth, and development. This is an exciting time in our lives!

Take a deep breath with me … Now, Let Us Begin!

Introduction

ॐ

**"Knowing yourself is the
beginning of all wisdom."**
- Aristotle[2] -

Picturing The Pieces

I want to begin a dialogue between us by asking you a few questions. I want you to visualize these questions. Visualization is a technique for creating mental images in order to comprehend and communicate a message. The steps are simple. The technique will begin with me asking you a few questions, then I will provide some guidance, and finally I will conclude the visualization.

So, why am I having you participate in this exercise?

I want you to start this journey with a level of clarity and understanding. It is important to acknowledge where you are and how you feel about where you are. Next, you can find out where you really want to be, and then take steps to your destination. My goal is to help you clearly see how you currently use and leverage the pieces in your life. I want you to be able to rearrange the pieces to create the life you want. Continue asking yourself questions as we go through this process. It is ok if your questions change.

Let's get started.

When you think about your life, what areas are in pieces?

Try not to over-think or over-complicate the question. The term "in pieces" means not whole, not complete, broken, shattered, or not fully arranged. I will be using the definition "not fully arranged" for the purpose of this book. When you read that question, can you think of one or more things that are in pieces?

If you focus internally, some examples are:

- o My **marriage** is in pieces.
- o My **family** is in pieces.
- o My emotional **well-being** is in pieces.
- o My **business** is in pieces.
- o My **health** is in pieces.
- o My **career** is in pieces.

If you focus externally, some examples are:

- o My **partner** is not …
- o My **children** are not …
- o My **employees** are not …
- o My **boss** is not …
- o If **this** would change, then I …
- o If **they** would change, then I …

We will talk about internal and external focus later. The important factor is that you personalize the question, and picture how the question looks to you. Now that you fully hear and understand the question, I want to present the question again. This time, I really want you to take a few moments to think about the question.

When you think about your life, what areas are in pieces?

Do you have that picture or those pictures yet? Good. There are no right or wrong answers in this process—only what is. I have another question for you.

How do those pieces make you FEEL?

When you picture your pieces, you feel a certain way. You may experience being shattered, broken, incomplete, or not whole. Again, that is perfectly fine. However, if you still do not know how to answer this question, let me help you.

Many of us think we have a "feeling" about a situation when, in fact, it is not really a feeling—it is an opinion. I want to know how **YOU** feel and not how **others** feel about your situation or "piece." I want to know how you **FEEL** and not your **opinion** about what you feel.

Example:

"I feel frustration." This is my feeling.

"I know I shouldn't be frustrated." That is an opinion about my feeling.

Now, you try it. Please write your answers in the "Placing Your Pieces" section of this chapter.

I "feel" _____. (feeling)
I think someone should _____. (opinion)

I "feel" _____. (feeling)
This is not right. I wish _____. (opinion)

I "feel" _____. (feeling)
Things could have been different if _____. (opinion)

I "feel" _____. (feeling)
I can or cannot make this work because _____. (opinion)

What is important here is that you know **what** you are feeling and not just the fact that you had a feeling. I am not interested in your opinion right now. In fact, as much as you are able, I want you to avoid having an opinion about the situation. Try to put it aside. You can pick up your opinion later if you want. For now, I want you to focus on how YOU feel. Does that make sense?

So again, how do those pieces make you **FEEL**?

Do you feel discomfort, disorganized, lost, hopeless, encouraged, challenged, optimistic, worried, confident …? Maybe you are experiencing a range of emotions. That is typical.

Now that you have pictured your pieces and the feelings that go along with those pieces, we can move on.

Thank you for doing this visualization with me.

As we conclude this visualization, I want to remind you that you are safe. You are secure. You are not alone in this journey even if you feel overwhelmed. You are ok. The answers that you seek are already present and will be revealed and understood more as we continue. You have everything it takes to build the life you want. I am here to help you uncover and unlock the tools you already possess and to use them more effectively.

I am committed to this journey with you. Commit to the process. Commit to yourself.

Knowing Yourself

Parenting is a mirror that is constantly reflecting the true you. Sometimes the mirror is your child. Other times, your own thoughts and actions mirror back to you who you are. These mirrors are tools which (by nature and purpose) fearlessly ask, **"What do you see?"** As parents, we see many things. We see things about our children that reflect joy. We see things about our children that reflect sorrow. We see life unfolding before us as it moves either to a desired creation or a growing frustration. Sometimes we reflect our best and sometimes our worst. Yes, this parental mirror is asking you, "What do you see?"

So, what **do** you see? Take a moment to answer. You have time.

What do I see about **parenting**?
What do I see about **my child**?
What do I see through **my expectations**?
What do I see about **my past**?
What do I see about **my present**?
What do I see about **my future**?

Feel free to add your own questions. Make these questions yours. Please write your answers in the "Placing Your Pieces" section of this chapter.

I believe all parents, at their core, want to make healthy decisions. I believe most parents want to positively affect their children. The question is, how do we make those decisions? The answer starts with you. The answer is found in your wisdom. Wisdom comes through many subjects and in many forms. I will focus on the kind of wisdom that comes from knowing yourself. I want you to become wise about who you are. I want you to benefit from the good that this wisdom produces. I often see three different kinds of people; ignorant people, idealistic people, and wise people.

An ignorant person is someone who does not seek to understand her/himself. This person rarely takes progressive actions, because s/he sees nothing that needs to change.

An idealistic person sees her/himself for what s/he hopes to be. This person often acts prematurely without the proper tools. This person sees the end result as more important than the process needed to achieve the goal.

A wise person seeks to know more about her/himself. A wise person simply sees things as they are and not as they would hope them to be. A wise person is not seeking something to change; a wise person seeks to comprehend. The desire of a wise person is in gaining knowledge no matter the source in which it comes. Because a wise person sees things for what they are, s/he uses that knowledge to make effective decisions. This person, at every step, is able to access a situation, identify the needs, and construct the path necessary for getting what they want.

Wise parents "bring forth" wise products. I want you to be able to do this. So, I want you to continually know yourself. You may want to jump directly to a list of rules about parenting. This is not where I will start. I will start where everything begins, and **everything begins with you**. All things start with knowing who you are. When you fully know yourself, you are a wise person.

Introduction

Throughout your path seek truth—know truth. Wise people seek truth and learn to apply it throughout life. Learning, using, and practicing your truth sets you free.

You are a wise person because you are reading this book. You did not find this book by accident. You have been seeking wisdom. You are on the journey of knowing yourself.

So, how does a person "know" themselves? Knowing yourself is the process of observing yourself. Begin to ask questions about your life and how you experience life around you. I will be asking you a lot of questions. Learn to love questions. Then, take the time to listen. Listen carefully because the·answer will come from you. It will come from within you. You will then have an answer.

Our perception of people and the intellectual prescriptions we give to people during their time of need is primarily based on our own personal knowledge and experiences. Parenting asks you to fulfill a need in someone else. Parenting will ask that you know another individual better than they even know themselves. And, how will you ever know another person if you do not know yourself? Therefore, the more you know of yourself, the more you are able to help others. The more you have experienced in your own life, the more helpful you can be to another. This is transference at its finest. Remember, we give to others what we have! We give to others who we are!

Introduction
Placing The Pieces

Based upon this chapter:

1: What are your broken pieces?

_____

_____

2: How do these pieces make you feel?

_____

_____ (feeling)

I think someone should

_____

_____ (opinion)

I "feel"

_____

_____ (feeling)

This is not right. I wish

_____

_____ (opinion)

Introduction

I "feel"

_____

_____ (feeling)

Things could have been different if

_____

_____ (opinion)

I "feel"

_____

_____ (feeling)

I can or cannot make this work because

_____

_____ (opinion)

3: What do you observe about yourself?

_____

_____

4: What do I "see" about parenting?

_____

_____

5:   What do I "see" about my child?

_____

_____

6:   What do I "see" through my expectations?

_____

_____

7:   What do I "see" about my past?

_____

_____

8:   What do I "see" about my present?

_____

_____

9:   What do I "see" about my future?

_____

_____

10:   What is working right now in your life?

_____

_____

11:   What is one thing you love about yourself?

_____

_____

12:   What is not working right now in your life?

_____

_____

13:   What is one way you can improve yourself?

_____

_____

Honor Yourself. *I acknowledge that I am doing well in some areas, and I agree to continually educate and improve myself where needed.*

_____   _____

Name   Date

Chapter 1

The PERSPECTIVE Piece

ଚ୍ଚ

"... One of the greatest gifts that we
give our children is our perspective.
... We model how to think."
- Steven Furtick[3] -

Puzzle Thoughts

Our family decided to take a trip to California's Redwood forest and stay at a cottage nestled on the aptly named "Avenue of the Giants." This was to be our first visit and our hopes were high. We drove our cozy car on the winding roads through the picturesque landscape. A warning had been issued to us (at our last stop) that this section of the trip did not sit well with children's stomachs. Sure that this concern did **not** apply to us, we sailed along the slippery roads taking in the majestic scenery. The rain tapped at the car windows and our children snuggled calmly in their car seats. Several of them dozed off, while our oldest wrote in his journal. I kept my eyes steadily on the road to avoid any slick spots and the promise of a crossing deer. Suddenly, a crude and familiar sound emanated from the back seat. My husband turned around with a panicked look on his face, and our collective sighs said it all. "Ughhhh."

We pulled the car over and ventured out in what was now sleet. Acting as a rescue team skilled in these kind of situations, we stripped our motion sick victim of his saturated clothes and quickly cleaned, dressed, and wrapped him in a warm blanket. My friend John, who used to work for the American Red Cross©, would have been proud of our emergency response and rescue skills. The car seat itself was beyond hope, and the thought of leaving it to the ravages of the elements did cross our minds more than once. Not being ones to burden nature with our trash, we did our best with baby wipes and extra towels. Finally, dripping wet and more than a little cold, we strapped everyone into the car and hobbled up the road. Our once oasis-like carriage now resembled a sanitation facility and the smell matched.

After several hours of driving, we arrived in the California Redwoods. The sight of our destination was more than a comfort, and the cabin staff were extra helpful. We started several loads of laundry and did our best to air out the car. We fed the boys, and they soon were crawling into bed where they instantly fell asleep. The adults sat by the fire, grateful for warmth and shelter. The front desk had taken pity. They showered us with board games and several 1,000 count puzzles. Wanting to spend some quality time with my husband and redeem some part of the night, I suggested we start on one of the puzzles. My husband hesitated but then quickly agreed. "Sure, why not?" We both laid out the pieces, and the idea for this book was born.

Steve Furtick (pastor of Elevation Church) states, "As fathers, we give gifts to our children. And, one of the greatest gifts, blessings, curses, or burdens that we give our children is our perspective. We pass on a perspective to our children. Far more than anything we'll teach them to do, they will learn from us—not what we say, but what we model—how to think—and specifically how to think about people."[4] Steve is exactly right. I would expand this statement to also include all parents (not just fathers). I love how perspective (one thought or one idea) can shift how we think and act.

While I sorted blue and brown puzzle pieces that cold and wintery night, I thought about the pieces that make up our lives. I had a different perspective at that moment than I did several years prior. I had different priorities and different goals. I reflected how I had gotten there. I was happy to be in that moment. I was thankful, despite our recent mishap. I thought about my journey from South Carolina to California. I thought about becoming a husband and a father. I thought about what might be in the future. What pieces were going to show up and what was the picture they would create?

Looking down at the jumbled puzzle parts scattered over the floor, it was hard to imagine that these pieces were going to create much of anything, let alone what was pictured on the box. I began the work. I had gotten a good section of our puzzle done. I was proud of myself. There was a slight competition between my husband and me. We are both competitive people and I, of course, saw myself as winning. But, there was this one piece I could not find. Much as I tried, I could not see a piece that fit the empty space. My head told me it was right in front of me, but my eyes told me otherwise. I must have mumbled something out loud because my husband gladly came to my rescue. He took one look at the pieces I had laid out in front of me and with an actual squeal of delight turned one of the puzzle pieces around and slipped it into place. He gloated as he returned to his side of the puzzle. "Thank You," I reluctantly said. I was more determined than ever.

What had just happened? **Perspective.**

I had been staring at the correct piece all along. I had probably even tried to force the piece into place upside down.

I just could not see what was right in front of me. I was looking at the pieces differently than my husband. Same piece, but with a different perspective. I am convinced that, with time, I could have found the fit. However, I desperately needed a shift in my perspective.

I would love to say that my puzzle assembling skills are much better after that experience. But at the time of writing this book, I have yet to test them again. However, the lesson is a good one. How can we shift our perspective to make the pieces of our life fit?

This book, as I mentioned in the preface, is about you. You are the puzzle master and, as such, you are the one sorting and putting together the picture of your life. You might at this moment be sitting (like I was) staring at an unfinished portion of your puzzle wondering how to make things work. If this is you, I invite you on a journey to shift your perspective. With your willingness to look at your puzzle with new and fresh eyes, and my insights I have collected over the years, we can fit the pieces together. Everything comes down to how you think. Parenting is no different.

Parenting is simply the outward product of your inward perspective.

Principles Not Policies

Having structure is the best thing that can happen to you. Not just structure with your children but I also mean for you.

Structure gives a framework upon which everything else is built. One of the reasons I believe it is important to focus on you, is that children are notoriously unstable. Building structure, for yourself, based solely on a child will fail. A child's will, wants, and moods change faster than water in a volcano. My goal is to give you the tools to build your own structure. From that structure, all the moving pieces can fit into place.

When most people hear the word structure, they immediately think of a set of rules. They think of regulations or dictates instituted by the parent for the child. Do not get me wrong. I am not saying you should get rid of rules. However, rules without relationship causes ruin. There is no easier way to destroy a relationship than having a laundry list of dos and don'ts. The truth is, policies sometimes create problems. Have you had the experience of returning an item to a store without the receipt?

I am pretty proactive when it comes to keeping receipts—especially for Best Buy©. This is probably my favorite store because I am a HUGE gadget geek. I keep receipts for budgeting purposes and for those rare occasions that I need to return an item. I know the potential frustrations of losing a receipt. I understand this through my previous retail work and by being "that" customer who "lost" their receipt. "Lost" meaning threw away.

I remember the last time I had to return an item to a well-known store. Not Best Buy©—I don't return gadgets. I do not remember if I had the receipt, BUT I do remember the experience. Whatever the situation was, the employee gave me an automatic response as to why she could not really assist me with the return. "I'm sorry sir. It's our policy." That has to be the worst phrase in all of retail.

"It's our policy," says many things but none that are positive or helpful in nature. Also, when others hear the word "policy" it can cause people to have several adverse and negative responses to you.

Why does this policy exist?
Who created this policy?
Why do you not want to help me?
Who can change or override this policy?
Rather than dictating a policy to me, figure out how to help me!

I have had many other experiences, where given the same circumstance, the retail clerk knew enough about the principle of the store to find a policy that really helped me. Sometimes this came in the form of finding a manager to override the policy. This perspective shift from policy-based actions to principles-based actions allows for flexibility. It allows us to answer the bigger question of why this policy was here to begin with. We also answer the even bigger question of "What does the store want?"

What does the store want? The store wants to sell merchandise to customers and make lots of money doing so. The store sees the need to function smoothly for both itself and its customers. In order to do this, polices are created. The store may automate its system, or the store may structure itself in other ways for maximum safety and profitability. When the automation or policy (in my case) goes against the very core of the store's larger goal (which is happy customers who keep buying and buying) we need to allow the system to be overridden or the policies need to be changed.

As a parent, I want you to try focusing on your core principles rather than a list of policies. This will set your perspective. Your principles will help guide you through any situation or problem that may arise with your child or with anyone else. Policies can change. Principles are stable. I want you to build the structure of your life on principles and not just on policies.

Chapter 1: The PERSPECTIVE Piece
Placing The Pieces

Based upon this chapter:

1: What are your principles?

_____

_____

2: What are your policies that support your principles?

_____

_____

3: Do you have any policies that conflict with your principles?

_____

_____

4: Do you have any policies that have nothing to do with your principles?

_____

_____

Honor Yourself. I acknowledge that I am doing well in some areas, and I agree to continually educate and improve myself where needed.

_____   _____

Name   Date

Chapter 2

The EXPECTATIONS Piece

಄

"Treat a man as he is and he will remain as he is.
Treat a man as he can and should be and
he will become as he can and should be."
- Stephen R. Covey[5] -

Can Be & Should Be

My husband and I had newly introduced our oldest two oldest children into our house. Our oldest boy was almost three at the time and his adjustment to us as foster/adoptive parents was understandably difficult. We expected and prepared for as much as we could. We prepared by going on numerous visits to where the boys were staying. We knew their sleeping and eating habits and we were starting to understand their personalities. We knew that our whole family was in for some adjustments once they actually moved in. We expected change.

Our expectations were met and exceeded. The first few months were particularly challenging as we got to know our oldest. He was going through a huge change. We were not what he was used to. He saw us as the enemy to all that was his "normal." We had been warned and had prepared for much of what we saw, but even so, it was very different living through the actual experience. Slowly our family started to stabilize and a new "normal" took shape—OUR normal. Our oldest son started to shift his opinion about us. We were not so bad. He started to try to copy us and assimilate us into his experience. This was a start. What I found interesting was the change in us. Because of our experiences with our son and because of who we were understanding him to be, we started to expect certain reactions or responses from him, and of course he expected certain reactions and responses from us.

I remember a conversation that my husband and I had one Sunday evening. We where talking about the progress of our son. My husband was quite burdened and voiced his concerns that we might never get our son out of his negative pattern of behavior. As I listened to him, I heard the fear and the sadness in his description of who he thought our son was. I stopped him and asked a question. Who do you want him to be? My husband paused. He had been so focused on the negative aspects of who our son was that he was losing sight of what he wanted for our son. He actually was losing sight of the other real and positive aspects of this young man. I gave him a challenge to raise his expectations for our son. I told him to try this for the next few weeks. Raise your expectations not your demands I told him. Keep your standards, but not your assumptions.

I received a phone call while driving to one of my classes I was teaching. It was my husband. He was like a giddy child. A week after my husband had taken my challenge, he was starting to see the first signs of change in our son. He started to see positive reactions to his positive expectations. My husband had made a choice to expect the best and in doing so, he made sure that he was not creating the worst. My son could sense the change and started to live up to the new expectations. Slow progress—yes—but it was progress nonetheless.

When you have gone through a lot of challenges in your life, it is very tempting to ignore, lower, and sometimes forsake your expectations. You may have heard someone say, "If you never have expectations, then you'll never be disappointed." All of humanity revolves around expectations. I know you have expectations. You expect to improve yourself by reading this book. You expect to feel accomplished as a parent. You expect to feel appreciated by your child. You expect for your child to grow up and maintain the principles you have taught them. You have expectations and that is good.

We all have expectations. Without expectations, we would be trapped in a whirlwind of instability and anxiety which would ultimately lead to our stagnation. We have expectations on every level of awareness—consciously, pre-consciously, sub-consciously, and unconsciously.

Take the operating of a vehicle, for example. Though you may not consciously think, "I'm going to get in the car, put the keys in the ignition and turn the car on," you certainly expect for the car to operate correctly. If you are sitting in a chair reading this book, you expect for the chair to remain intact and not collapse. These are subtle, yet powerful ways in which we experience our expectations in every day life.

There is a concept in philosophy and spirituality called the "law of firsts." It is often referred to as the "law of first mention." This law simply means that when something is mentioned for the first time, that theme (or that idea) is carried throughout everything moving forward. It is a sign of what is to follow. Think of it as a governing principle of what you may experience.

The potency of any subject really comes from two ingredients—expectation and perspective.

The EXPECTATIONS Piece

I will talk later in this book about stress and pain, but I am going to mention pain now as an example of how expectations can develop.

We started out our early existence here in this physical form with this thing we call pain. Because it is a "first mention" we have thought that pain is supposed to direct us and lead us. Just because pain was one of our first experiences does not mean that pain is meant to control, rule, or be our friend. I want you to unlearn your expectation of pain. I am going to ask you to shift your perspective and expectation on other topics as well. What you expect from pain—for example—lets your mind, body, and soul know what to do with pain. What you expect from pain, lets you know how much to receive from pain and how to respond to pain.

Do you have the expectation that all pain is bad? If so, you will receive all of the bad things and typically abort the learning lesson in the process. Do you believe that all pain is meant to harm you or is a result of something bad you have done? If so, you will tend to be more defensive and instead of seeing an opportunity for growth, you will view pain as another reason you have failed. Even though pain is a pattern that repeats itself in our lives, it does not have to bring about negative responses and results. It does not have to hold negative expectations. We will get more into this later.

A shift of perspective and expectation works with any topic.

We all live up to the expectations set for us. Likewise, others live up to the expectations that we set for them. As a parent, I want you to think bigger than you have currently been thinking. I want you to start now charting a course with newly refined expectations. These expectations will not be solely based upon what you have always experienced but on the possibilities that lie ahead.

Living fully and freely is about expecting great things. All things begin in our mind. Your thinking is the material upon which you build your life. What condition are your materials in? Are the conditions of your "mental material" corroding? Are they brittle? Let's recondition these materials and start anew.

What "Can Be" in your life? For your family? I do not want you to merely think about how things are right now. I want you to free yourself and your family. All things are possible. We want to reinforce healthy patterns and keep from repeating trauma. As you continue thinking about what you have always had, you will continue to receive that very thing. When we think about the things that "can be" in our lives it invokes something or someone's potential.

Yes, we are going to take action on these thoughts, but right now I want you to dream. What "Should Be" in your life? You should be happy. You should be successful. You should be proud of yourself and the accomplishments you are making as a parent. **You** make up your own "Should Be" expectations. And then, once you have done that, turn them into "Will Be" statements. Set these new thoughts as your intention and your perspective. See your piece from a different angle. You will start to see change.

Our expectations are always made manifest on the wings of possibility. Anything and everything is possible. Believe.

Adjusting Your Expectations

Do not abolish your expectations; simply adjust your expectations.

I have actively adjusted my expectations regarding parenting. I definitely had to adjust what I expected to "feel" when I became a parent and what I wanted to get out of my parenting experience. When I think back, I sometimes find it difficult to reclaim the thoughts that I had about parenting before I was a parent. I do remember that my current reality does not match my former expectations.

If you do not have children now, what do you think parenting will feel like to you? What is your expectation? If you currently have children, are your feelings about parenting different from what you imagined they would be?

How do we shift our expectations?

I am going to talk about several different ways to parent. Watch how they apply to your expectations. I believe most parents fall into one of these categories or a combination of these categories. The categories I will describe are Contrast, Compensation, Conversion, and Competition.

1:   The CONTRAST Category
"I'm going to give my child all the things and the experiences that I did not have."

You become a parent to rebel against the experiences of your childhood. This is expressed in terms like:

> When I become a parent I'll never ...
> When I become a father I'm going to ...
> When I am a parent my child will ...
> When I am a mother I ...

This kind of parenting is externally parent-focused. Even though the Contrast category is parent-focused, it is not focused on **you** as the parent but actually other parents—in this case **your** parents. This is often expressed as doing the opposite of everything your parents did. You are trying to parent from a place of contrast. The expectation is aimed at being a better parent to your children than your parents were to you. You might have forgiven your parents. However, forgiving is not always forgetting. Because you remember what was done to you, you often vow to not repeat the problem. But this focus may, in fact, do that very thing. The Contrasting category often views your parents as able to provide but *unwilling* to do so, and this kind of parenting is often met with hostile feelings such as anger and bitterness.

2: The COMPENSATION Category
"I'm going to give my child all the things and the experiences that I wanted."

You become a parent in order to fill in the missing gaps that your parents could not fill. This is expressed in terms like:

My parents never took me to _____ so ...

I wish my parents would have _____ so ...

As a child, I always wanted _____ so ...

I never got to _____ so ...

This is very similar to the Contract category but with a slight twist. The Compensation category views your parents as *unable* to provide *but willing* to do so and this kind of parenting is met with feelings such as empathy and understanding. This is where you understand that your parents simply could not provide the things and experiences they wanted to. They could not provide due to social or economic situations and not because of neglect. The Compensation category is externally child-focused. In this parenting style you try to live vicariously through your child's life. Victories for your child are really victories for you. Failures for your child are really failures of you as the parent. Because you did not get certain experiences as a child or adult, you are trying to get a second chance through your child's life.

3: The CONVERSION Category
"I'm going to give my child all the things and the experiences that I had."

You become a parent to repeat the experiences of your childhood. This is expressed in terms like:

When my child gets old we will _____ just like I remember …

My child and I will _____ just like my parents did with me …

Because I loved this when I was younger, I want my child to …

This parenting style is also externally child-focused, and again, you try to live vicariously through your child. The Conversion category is often expressed by trying to make your child relive all **your** childhood experiences because your childhood was filled with love, safety, belonging, quality relationships, and happiness. And because you remember all of your wonderful experiences, you force your child to have a "thriving" childhood. This is often done with good intentions, but ultimately you are trying to convert your child into someone s/he is not. You will not allow them to have their own experiences. You have little regard for your child as an individual, and you potentially introduce trauma in her/his life by going against who your child is as an individual.

4: The COMPETITION Category
"I'm going to give my child all the things and the experiences that others do not have."

You become a parent to express your ability to parent "better" and "more effectively" than other parents. This is expressed in terms like:

> When I become a parent my child is going to achieve …
> My child will never act like …
> I'm going to make sure my child knows more than …

This expression of parenting has a component of the Contrast category, but it takes it one step further. Instead of focusing on the point of parental contrast we broaden our focus to include the child. It is actually a combination of Contrast and Conversion. Now this parenting is child-focused and parent-focused. Focused on the right child (yours) but the wrong parent. Focused on the child but for the wrong purpose. Oftentimes the parent is trying to "keep up with the Jones'." Your goal is to be the best family on the block. Your expectation is to have the best of everything and be seen as the best—it is a Competition. The purpose in the Competition category is to conquer other parents. The Competition category can also show up in divorces where the focus is on the former partner. This is very dangerous, since you are using your child as a weapon against the other parent. When you think like this, you put a great deal of pressure on the child's performance, but they will never live up to your expectations.

I know, I have personally been in many of these categories. I did not always think I was, and it took me quite a while to even admit it—but I was.

Nobody is blaming you for reacting to the negative things in your life. No one is condemning you for rebelling. Every good child becomes a rebel at some point. Your child will be a rebel at some point too. Get Ready! Be Prepared! Make sure your wine cellar is full. We have often joked in our house that when children become rebellious it's God's and Karma's way of saying, "HAHA, this is payback for what you did to your parents." There may be some truth to that. All that to say, there is a valid explanation for every form of rebellion. I am not saying that it feels good to be on the receiving end of rebellion—I am just saying that it is a part of parenthood.

I remember how I rebelled against my father. I learned the following;

1. Keep Your Promises
2. Keep Your Commitments
3. Take Responsibility For Your Actions

In my life it has always been my mom and me. I remember seeing my dad (what felt like) around five times during the course of my life. When I was younger, he would take me to get my haircut at Frankie Chatten's Barber Shop in Chatham, Virginia. I have very fond memories of going there and when I am in the area, I try to stop by to say hello to Mr. Chatten. I remember on one occasion, after getting my haircut, my dad took me to a local shop and he bought me a teddy bear. Now, this was not just any teddy bear. This was Teddy Ruxpin™—a singing and talking animatronic bear that was pretty popular in the 80's. Everyone wanted a Teddy Ruxpin™, and if your parents "really loved you" it was yours. Apparently, my dad "really loved me" and he bought me one.

That Teddy Ruxpin™ bear was the first and only gift I ever received from my dad when I was a child. The second and last gift I received from my dad, as a young adult, was a Dell™ laptop that he gave me while I was in college. After years of not talking to him, I figured out how to get in touch with him, and I convinced him that I needed a laptop for my foreign exchange trip to Germany.

As a child, I remember getting calls from him when he was incarcerated. For those of us old enough to remember, when you called someone long distant, you had the option of charging the call to the recipient. Of course, the recipient had to accept, but it was a convenient way of making long distant phone calls when you did not have the money to pay for the call. This was especially true in the jail and prison systems.

There is an interesting type of trauma that occurs when you know your parent is in jail and you receive a call saying, "You have a collect call from {insert name}. Will you accept this call?" No matter how sweet the automated attendant sounds, it is not the type of call that infuses peace and hope in your life. I think the trauma is magnified when you are the child receiving the call from your incarcerated parent. Think of the subconscious messages that are conveyed:

1. You are separated from your parent; the barrier always exists.
2. Someone else controls communication between you and your parent.
3. Your parent is the only one that can initiate communication.
4. If communication is not initiated, your parent did not want it.
5. Your parent is making you "pay" for communication.
6. You have the responsibility of "accepting" communication no matter the form or time.
7. Communication and connection has an end so get it when you can.

When my father did call me from jail, which was rare, he would ALWAYS make promises to me.

"Brian, (which is what my family calls me) I'm coming to visit you and your mom when I get out."

"Brian, I'm going to take you to get a haircut when I get out."

"Brian, I'm coming in town this weekend and will come by to see you."

These were my least favorite promises. One of the blessings and curses of growing up in a small town is that everyone knows your name, but everyone also knows your business. So, when my dad would come into town, he would see everyone else but me. Within a couple of hours or days, someone who knew my father would eventually tell me, "Hey, I saw your dad this weekend. He came over the house and he said he was coming to see you. Did you see him?" The answer was always, "No, I didn't."

After having this happen more than I care to remember, I vowed that I would always keep my promises, always keep my commitments, and always take responsibility for my actions—no matter what. I grew up consistently thinking that something was wrong with me. Surely, I am doing something wrong. Maybe if I do "this" he will change. The fact was that I could not change him; I could only change myself. I can alter my expectations of him and yet keep my standards for me. I learned that I would not receive love and affection from him but that I was worthy of love and affection from others. I learned to expect the things I wanted but learned to receive them from different sources. This one secret helped save me much pain over the years. **Learning how to adjust your expectations will save you from unnecessary grief.**

So when it came time to parent, I was not going to be like my dad. I promised myself that I would always be there for my kids, and I would show them love. I did this by wanting to buy them a lot of things. I was Contrast parenting. You should have seen our first Christmas. You would have thought that we were actually in Santa's workshop. The toys were piled high. This was not for my children; this was for me and for my husband who was doing Compensation parenting. We both, for different reasons, wanted to give them what we never had.

I have learned to balance myself out over the years although I still really like to buy stuff for my kids. Now, when I buy them something, I do it because **I want to** not because I have to outdo my father.

My interactions with my boys the first few years tended to be about forcing them to have the opposite feelings, emotions, and experiences that I had. I found myself, all too often, reliving my life through my children. I put a lot of pressure on them to accept and love me. And, what child really loves their parent(s) all the time? Be honest. This was unfair to them and to me. They would come to love me over time as we got to know each other. But, they did not love me **because** of my father. They have never met my father. They loved me for me, which is the way it should be.

When I was in my Contrast, Conversion, Compensation, and Competitive parenting and I saw that my children were resistant to me as a parent, I felt defeated. I was a "bad" parent just like my dad. This had nothing to do with my actual parenting or the actual relationship I had with my children. The truth was I was doing a great job and had a very healthy relationship with my children. I was just trying to relive my experiences through my children which was impossible. I was trying to fix me through my children. I was trying to fix my relationship with my father through my children. I also was trying to conquer my father by Contrast and Competition parenting. I realized quickly I did not want to use my children against my father. Once I realized I was doing this, I told myself, "The cycle stopped with me." I loved my children too much to parent from any perspective other than a healthy and thriving one.

I am more aware of who I am as a person now and, as such, do not need to rebel against my dad. My dad has less and less impact on my life as I grow more and more into my true Self. I can take the things I learned from my dad and adjust them into something positive. Without my dad I most likely would never have learned to keep my promises or commitments. I never would have learned so clearly to take responsibility for my actions had it not been for him. I am able to help hundreds of other people **because** of my dad. I have no lack, only different pieces. I am thankful.

I spent YEARS reaching out to my dad. I spent years begging for a relationship that, quite honestly, he did not want. After years of silence, I came to the resolution that the "failure" of this parent-child relationship was not my fault. I also learned that some of the most dangerous relationships in the world are obligatory relationships. Every relationship must be defined. This must be done by all parties involved. Many times we do not define what we expect from relationships. This is true especially with the relationships we feel obligated to such as our parents, family members, and friends.

When you do not define your expectations, you give your puzzle over to another. And, whatever is created will be up to them. You invite others to control, rule, or destroy your life—even if they are well meaning people. You are the only one who knows how and what your life should look like. No one—other than you—should be arranging your pieces. Allowing others to do your work because of undefined boundaries or expectations invites hurt feelings and regret.

You need to know your expectations for yourself, your child, and the people that are supporting you on this journey. You need to know how to shift those expectations if they are not working for you. I am not saying to do this out of revenge or frustration. I am saying shift all your own pieces to work for your own puzzle. This is you-focused. Everything else will fall into place.

So what kind of parenting should you be striving for?

5.   The RESOURCE Category
"I am going to do the best I can with the resources I have."

This kind of parenting takes the strengths of the parent and combines them with the strengths of the child, community, family, or any other elements and creates a stable healthy environment while promoting the combined safety and growth of all involved. This kind of parenting is internally parent-focused. In other words, this kind of parenting is You-focused—which is perfect. This is where you know You as a parent. You know your genius and identity—which we will talk about more. You know what resources as a parent you have inside you and those resources you need from your community.

You are parenting from a secure and stable perspective and not for or against anyone else.

This is where it all comes together. Many pieces moving and interacting in concert with each other. Not one piece better than the other, but all understanding their role, their place, and their contribution. This is life; ever shifting, changing, and growing. There is not one right way to be a resource to yourself or your child. The best thing you can do for your child is be a conduit of resources that the child can choose from. And it is fine if you cannot provide something for your child. You direct them to someone or something that has the answers your child is looking for. You are not supposed to be all the answers for your child. You are there to guide and direct them. Being the best You is more than enough.

After not hearing from my father for years, I reached out to him again when I was living in South Carolina. By this time, I had spent much time grieving the loss of my absentee father. I accepted the fact I did not have a father and came to a resolution that I was still interested in having a relationship with this 'stranger' I was supposed to call dad. We began a series of healthy and mutually beneficial conversations over the course of a couple of weeks. Those good conversations quickly turned into grieving conversations where my dad spent most of the time apologizing for not being more present in my life. While part of me appreciated receiving the apologies, another part of me felt awkward. The conversations started feeling like I was parenting my father and helping to release the guilt of his actions. This is when I knew the conversations were taking the wrong turn. The conversations continued for a while and then … silence … again. After a couple of months he called me back. I remember this call vividly. I felt the clearest I had ever felt up until that point. The phone rang. I looked at the phone. It was him. I answered the phone. This time I remained silent.

"Brian?" he said.

I curiously said, "Yes?"

"You sound like you don't want to hear from me," he replied.

I took a bold move in defining the expectations of our relationship.

I told him, "It's not that I don't want to hear from you, it's just I'm confused why you called me. My friends call me. My family calls me. People that love me, call me. Strangers don't call me."

Obviously angry from the comment, my dad then hung up the phone. So, being the person that I am, I called him right back and I led the conversation. I was setting my boundaries. I respectfully let him know that I did not appreciate him hanging up on me. As two adults, we should be able to have a discussion in a mature manner. I also told him that the reality is I do not know anything about him and he has not volunteered any information either. The last conversations have been nothing more than therapy sessions for him.

The EXPECTATIONS Piece

I ended the conversation with an open invitation and I said, "I want nothing more than to have a relationship with you but things need to change. I released you from the obligation of being my father a long time ago. I'm ok and you're ok. If you want to be in my life, you need to build a relationship with me just like everyone else. If you want to do that then great! If that's not what you really want, I understand and we should move on."

I knew that I could not fix him and that I could not allow myself to be used to cleanse his conscience. I had suffered enough of an unhealthy dynamic between the two of us. Moving forward we needed to have a clear directive focused on healthy growth.

He said, "Ok, and I wish you well in your life."

I paused. He was offering nothing more. I said, "You too."

That was the last conversation I had with my dad.

I have never looked back. I love my dad for what he taught me. I love him as a person and as a fellow human being. However, I have a very clear and well-defined foundation. I know who I am and am learning more about me every day. I respect myself and love myself enough to know my genius. I have a perspective that is self-focused and willing to shift as I change and grow. My identity is strong and continues to grow as I expand and develop. I have less stress in my life because I know where I am and can easily distinguish between perceived and actual threats. I choose responses that are balanced and well-informed so as to bring myself back into alignment and health. I use the pieces I have and place them in the spaces that best serve me. I know that I will have each piece I need when the time is right. I can see clearly. I am never in lack. I am creating the picture that I love, and I am having fun doing it. I am using all the internal and external resources I have to parent my children, and I know this is more than enough.

I have done this. I know you can too.

Chapter 2: The EXPECTATIONS Piece
Placing The Pieces

Based upon this chapter:

1: What "should be" in your life?

_____

_____

2: What "will be" in your life?

_____

_____

3: What are your strengths as a parent?

_____

_____

4: What resources do you have in your community?

_____

_____

5: What expectations do you have for yourself?

_____

_____

6: What expectations do you have for your child(ren)?

_____

_____

7: How might shifting your expectations help you?

_____

_____

Honor Yourself. *I acknowledge that I am doing well in some areas, and I agree to continually educate and improve myself where needed.*

_____   _____

Name   Date

Chapter 3

The GENIUS Piece

೫౧

"Something within you cannot be found in another ...
If you do not know your distinctive difference,
you will never discern what others need from you."
- Mike Murdock[6] -

You Are Unique

Adoption had always been my husband's first choice when it came to starting a family. I, however, explored all options and agreed adoption was best for us only when I had weighed the pros and cons of each decision. Once agreed, we moved to a new and larger apartment. We took the necessary classes, and we readied our home for the children we dreamed of having. Furniture was bought, supplies were stockpiled, and anticipation mounted. We waited for that phone call. My husband occupied his time painting a mural in what would be the children's room. Christmas came and left, and we still waited. This gave us plenty of time to think about what kind of parents we hoped and wanted to be. Resting at the foundation of all our self-reflection was this basic question—were we able to be good parents?

My questions stemmed from being raised by a single mother who, despite being a capable individual, could never show me how to be my father. I knew who my father was but I did not "know" him. My own father's absence gave me a "missing" piece, and I was left to create this piece on my own. I would later discover a different perspective on the idea of "missing." However, at the time, I had the perspective a piece **was** missing. Like I said before, I found myself often crafting the "father" piece solely based on doing the opposite (contrast parenting) of what my father did. I knew better. I knew that I should be creating from what I **wanted** to be as a father instead of what I did **not** want to be as a father. I knew I should be looking for my personal father piece and not searching for my biological father's piece. I had developed a strong sense of who I was in every other area of my life. However, in regard to being a father, I needed time to build my confidence in what I could and would do. Was I going to be good father?

My husband's questioning came from the opposite spectrum. He had a father. He experienced a full childhood. Taking trips, having long talks with his father, and watching his father work was his childhood norm. My husband placed pressure on himself to "live up to" his father. He was searching for a duplicative piece. He wanted to copy his father. Then, as it turned out, he "lost" even that piece. You see, when my husband was a young adult, his parents divorced. His father left to start another family. A father that he once knew, now was a stranger to him. The feeling of isolation and rejection was further compounded when my husband came out as being gay. Rejection from his father was firmly cemented. So on the one hand, he wanted to copy his father's piece, and yet on the other hand, he felt he was missing his father's piece. My husband constantly asked himself doubting questions. Would he be able to be the father he had? Would he abandon his children too? Would he love his children even when they did something he didn't like? The questions came in different forms but they were the same. Was he going to be a good father?

What we both learned from our soul searching was that we were not our fathers. We were not our mothers. We were not anyone but ourselves. Yes, we learned from others along the way, but our choices were **ours.** The gifts and tools we had to offer were ours alone. We were unique.

Parents have thoughts that are cluttered with the doubt of their abilities. We doubt our ability to provide what our children need. We doubt our ability to love. We doubt our ability to teach. We doubt our ability to _____. You fill in the blank. The list goes on and on and is as varied as the parents thinking the thoughts. Parents have been made to believe that they must be some kind of super-being. They have to be a super-hero with super powers. God forbid they were born a human like the rest of us. Surely, if they were human, they would be doomed to be less-than-successful as a parent. We have put so much pressure on parenthood that it is a wonder many still want to be parents. You may have bought into this notion that parenting is about doing everything at the same time and doing it perfectly. You may have tried to be the hero. You may believe that you have to be there for your child at every step of the way or else you have failed. You may have told yourself that if you mess up, you will damage your child for life. We doubt our abilities based upon so many factors that are external of ourselves when the real answers lie within us. So why do we doubt ourselves?

Most of these kind of feelings about who a parent should be or what a parent should do are misguided at best. They come from a belief that we as parents have to be the collective sum of all the good examples that came before us or conversely that we have to avoid all the poor examples we have seen in others. This definition of parenthood has failure built in. Sadly, this line of thinking shows up not only in parenting but in many aspects of our lives. Any time we take the examples of others and assume that we must be all of who they were or who they were not, we will find ourselves lost and feeling like a failure. You cannot be everyone else and be you at the same time. Those examples are just that—examples. What you do with those examples and how you use your own unique skills to enhance those examples only you can decide.

Fearful or stressful ideas of parenthood are usually us responding negatively to someone else's opinion—an opinion which, against our true nature, we have made our own. This is why in our earlier exercise I wanted you to focus on the feeling you had and not the opinion you had about the feeling. What was good for them may not be good for you. What made them unique will not make you unique.

Take, for example, making tea. My husband had an aunt who made (according to him) the best spiced tea ever. He was determined that our family was going to carry on a spiced tea tradition. So come Christmas, he set out to replicate his aunt's tea. He could have gone to the source, but since he and his aunt were not on speaking terms after he "came out," he was on his own. He decided to test different recipes that claimed to be the tea he remembered. The tea making began. Batch after batch of what I thought was perfectly good tea was frowned upon by my husband's scrupulous taste buds. The truth was, we were never going to find a perfect match. I knew this but I could not tell him. My husband felt like a tea making failure and he still might have felt this way even with the original recipe. He was not his aunt and there was little he could do to live up to the standard of tea making that he thought was her's. Her standard, be it true or fictitious, was impossible to achieve.

She was unique in her tea making. My husband was trying to replicate his aunt instead of letting her be the expert in tea.

What I knew of my husband was that he was excellent at creating family experiences. He knew just the right way to make us feel special with his own pieces. He could take a bit of this and a tad of that and mix it together to create a feeling of warmth and home. He was fine without his aunt's tea. What he lacked was confidence. He had all the answers inside him. I knew that, but did he?

How many times do we feel we need to be someone else? How many times do we feel we need to parent like someone else? Parenting, as I will explain, is about knowing what you do well and constantly improving on it. Parenting is about knowing what your unique pieces are. And when you know what your special brand of parent is, then you work with those pieces to be a more effective parent. Adding someone else's piece to your puzzle is only going to confuse and frustrate you. And the picture you create with someone else's mismatched piece will create a picture that is just that—mismatched.

Albert Einstein[7] said, "The difference between stupidity and genius is that genius has its limits." I agree. The word "limit" can seem negative, but it does not have to be. Let me substitute the word "edge." A helpful strategy in constructing puzzles is to find the edges. I first look for the corners. I also look for flat-edged pieces. I do this so that I can start to frame the picture that I am creating. This gives me a reference—a boundary if you will—a limit. Once I know the limits/edges of the puzzle I can work inside the puzzle to create and complete the picture. There is a comfort and a freedom that comes from knowing that your puzzle has edges. The point being made is that you need to know where you begin and where you end. You need to know who you are and that you are unique. I want you to know your edges, or know the unique pieces that make you—You.

How can we find our edge? One of the strongest and most natural way to find our edge is to compare and contrast. As a parent, you look for examples and advice almost any place you can get it. This is good. Seeking information from many sources is an indicator that you take your parenting seriously. But, I am going to give a word of caution. Comparing and contrasting is supposed to be used to help us decide what we want. However, when we look for answers outside of ourselves, the conversation of comparison and contrast can turn to "you **versus** them." Another way to say this is "you **against** them." When I was younger I saw this conversation clearly.

I remember surveying relationships and family dynamics while growing up in Virginia. I have always been an inquisitive and observant person. I was raised in a predominantly black community and in a single parent home. Single parent homes were almost the family signature of my community. I rarely remember seeing a family with two parents. Outside of our community—yes. Within our community—no. Occasionally there was an exception but it was rare. I observed women having to be both caregiver and provider in our community. Other communities shared this responsibility. I noticed that it was too easy in our community for men to get women pregnant and then leave because they did not want—or felt they could not handle—the responsibility. I saw something different with other communities. There was a lot to compare and contrast.

We were literally on the "the other side of the tracks" but of course this idea went beyond the physical. There was a racial, social, and economic divide in our town. It was not always so simple as the whites were on one side (the good side) and blacks were on the other side (the bad side). But the white and more affluent "seemed" to have more than our black and more impoverished communities. However, no matter how clear or unclear the division might have been, the **contrasts** were quite obvious.

Likewise so were the **comparisons**. I was *black* so that meant I should dress and act a certain way. I was supposed to vote for a certain political party. I was supposed to listen to certain music and like certain food. I was expected to have faith in what they had faith in. I was expected to love the same things my community loved and have the same values my community had. I was compared to them because of my origin and my looks. This comparison had nothing to do with who I **was** but who I **seemed** to be based upon people that physically looked like me.

Is there value in this process of comparison and contrast? Yes there is. I see value as it is applied to knowing what you do want and knowing what you do not want. I see value in these types of conversations if (and only if) they can help you define and refine who you are as a person. What do you want? Who do you want to be? What do you want to achieve in and of yourself? Comparisons and contrasts beyond this use can do more harm than they can good. Everything goes down to your intent.

When we compare and contrast ourselves to others with the intent of bettering ourselves, we find positive results that yield more effective ways of parenting. When we compare and contrast ourselves to others through the lens of inadequacy, we often initiate a process of doubt, negative self-criticism, and low self-esteem. This type of negative thinking only highlights all the things we are doing wrong (with no solutions) and less of the things we are doing right.

I started at an early age to hold such conversations about my life and my family with others; not with the intent of growing, but with the intent of exposing circumstances that seemed unfair. It was not fair that my dad was in jail more than he was at home. It was not fair that some families were able to go on vacation and we could not. It was not fair that ...

I had this **family.**
I had this **life.**
I had this **parent.**
I had this **community.**
I was **me.**

Having these conversations most often has more to do with who you **aren't** as opposed to who you **are**; what you **lack** as opposed to what you **have**. We think something or someone else can give us information, opportunity, or instruction that we see as missing. Again, we think we have a missing piece. I call this polluting your picture.

I am not trying to get you to avoid all comparing and contrasting of yourself as a parent to other parents. And, used positively, comparing and contrasting is a great tool. You can use the art of comparison and contrast to find your piece. But, comparing does not have to be polluting. What is the difference between progressive comparisons and contrasts, versus polluted comparisons and contrasts?

Progressive comparisons and contrasts are when you can look at someone else, see the good things they are doing, and try to integrate their principles into your life because *they fit your life.* You do not view them as a threat but as an ally to your overall success. They help you find your own pieces and show you clever ways to quickly and effectively bring your puzzle together.

What are polluted comparisons and contrasts? This is when we allow other things and people to add their piece to our puzzle. Instead of helping us find our pieces, we allow and help them force their piece into our picture. Polluted comparisons lead to the corruption of our puzzle. When you use this method, you gradually neglect the purpose you have in this life. You are changing the essence of your own puzzle. You are no longer the puzzle master of your own life. Over time, this erosion of your inner Self begins to take its toil until your very foundation is in jeopardy.

Let me say this another way. We have referenced internal and external sources but let me take some time to clearly lay out what I am talking about. What do I mean by external verses internal? Simply put, when I talk about something external, I am talking about anything that comes from outside you. That could be a thought, an action, a feeling, an opinion, or any combination of those things. When I talk about something being internal I am talking about anything that is purely from you. Pure, clean, and solely from your ideas, thoughts, emotions, and desires—all the parts that make up you.

Much talk is given to who we are. So who is doing the talking? Everyone! Almost every teacher, philosopher, and person with a voice and influence has probably told you what you should or should not do. Even this book is an external source giving you thoughts for you to sift through. External sources are not bad but they are not us. We can use something external to our benefit if we know that it matches up with something that is already internal. This is a good use of external. Taking the external and using it to our benefit is wonderful. There is nothing wrong with using external sources to bolster and help us along our way. The problem arises only when we confuse the external source as being internal. This is especially dangerous when the external source does not fit our own internal source. We get confused and derailed. Allowed long enough, this system of operating will drown out our true identity. I want you to always start internally and then work externally. You are in control of you.

PARENTING WITH PIECES

My husband had been a parent for several years. His heart was big and his goals for himself were high. He scheduled and planned and shuttled our kids about, giving them opportunity after opportunity. He got up early and went to bed late. Sometimes I would come home in the afternoon to find him crashed on the bed exhausted from the stress of his parenting. We talked about ways to lighten his burden but nothing seemed to work. He grew more and more impatient and frustrated with the kids but mostly with himself. One afternoon we were in the kitchen, and we had a conversation while the kids were taking a nap. He said to me, "I feel so angry all the time, and I don't know why. I don't like this feeling, and I don't want it to be a part of my life." I asked him why he thought he had to do all of these things that he was doing. I pointed out that if these activities or methods were causing him so much stress then maybe he shouldn't do them. And if he was going to continue with everything that was on his plate, then he needed to find a way to do these activities without frustration.

I could tell the resistance he had toward what I was saying. He went through the reasons why he "had" to do these things. Slowly he started to smile. The more he defended his position the more he knew it was not even a position that he wanted to hold. Then the breakthrough. He turned to me and let out a big sigh. "I think I am parenting for my mother." He looked both relieved and horrified at the same time. We went on to talk about why he felt he needed to parent the way his mother would have parented. Why he felt the need to gain approval from a person who had not been in his life for several years. The answers were simple. Down at the root of everything was an internal need trying to be filled with external source. He missed his mom and wanted her to say he was doing a good job. He was asking for something outside of himself. Something he knew he was not going to get. This fueled his frustration and spilled out into the lives of the people he loved the most. This clearly was not working.

While looking at others to see how they parent may have value, please realize that you are a different person. You have different children. You have different needs and wants. You have different circumstances. You have different goals and principles. Knowing the difference between external parenting (working outside your borders) and internal parenting (working inside your borders) will save you a lot of trouble. I am here to tell you that you are unique. There is no parent exactly like you and there never will be. We do not want there to be. So while you may not be like the rest of the parents, you are You. You are a new and special picture all on your own. That is enough. Knowing your limits puts you in the genius category. Knowing your limits allows you to focus on your strengths. Genius is about knowing your unique value and bringing that value into every situation.

You Have What It Takes

Parenthood starts with your pattern of thinking. The way you think about yourself is the key. I want to encourage you that you do have what it takes. You Are A Genius.

So, what again is this genius I keep talking about? Let's review. A genius is a person with exceptional ability or capacity usually in a specific area. We have learned how genius knows its boundaries and unique abilities. Genius also makes an informed decision at every stage and transition.

What are the areas as a parent where you thrive? This is your place of genius. Your genius, or unique identifying quality, is the bedrock of stability and success. This is where you find your principles to build your parenthood. You are a genius; not in the making, but in the here and now. You simply need to accept it. No amount of classes, education, or experience can give you what you already possess. Education simply enhances who you already are. There is nothing you need to do to become greater than you already are in this moment. You need only respect this truth and accept this truth as your own.

What I want you to start hearing is that you have pieces. Yes, that is a good thing. You have "stuff" to work with. No, your piece is not the same as the other person. Yes, it might be smaller or bigger. But you do have pieces. Out of pieces you can start to create. I want you to start looking at these pieces as possibilities. Neither you nor I know exactly what you are going to create. However, I do know only you can do the creating. Instead of looking at all these pieces as failures and problems look at them as endless opportunities to find the beautiful work of art you want to share with the world. And even if you do not know where everything fits—it is ok. You do not have to know everything right now. You will know what to do with each piece when you need to know. You will find the right fit when it is the right time. Yes, sometimes the pieces will flow into place almost like a magnet is pulling them together. And other times there will be a hunt for a piece that you just cannot seem to find. I can assure you that there are no missing pieces. And when we feel like there is a missing piece, as in the case of my "father" piece, I can tell you from experience that you have everything you need. We are only missing a piece when compared to someone else's puzzle. We must remind ourselves that our picture is not theirs and their picture is not ours. Shifting your perspective on this will allow you to find your unique genius-piece.

The skills you need for parenting will always appear when you need them. Sometimes you just need to practice patience. I know those are not words we love to hear in this society of instant gratification, but instant results are not always lasting results. You are seeking to be a genius, not simply to be gratified.

The great Italian sculptor, painter, and poet of the High Renaissance, Michelangelo, once said, "Genius is eternal patience."[8] I believe Michelangelo, who undoubtedly influenced the development of Western Art, knew this principle first hand. You will grow in patience as you are developing the living art that is your family. This is not always instant. With patience you will get there. Continue believing in yourself and your genius will shine through.

Chapter 3: The GENIUS Piece
Placing The Pieces

Based upon this chapter:

1: How are you unique?

_____

_____

2: How does this show through in your parenting?

_____

_____

3: What are some good examples others have given you?

_____

_____

4: What are the positive lessons you want to remember from these good examples?

_____

_____

5: What are some poor examples others have given you?

_____

_____

6: What are some positive lessons you want to remember from these poor examples?

_____

_____

7: Describe to yourself areas you allow external forces to influence you?

_____

_____

8: What internal ideas do you have?

_____

_____

9: How are you going to focus on you internally?

_____

_____

10: Are there any internal or external ideas you want to change?

_____

_____

11: What kind of borders or limits have you created?

_____

_____

12: Tell me and yourself reasons you have what it takes.

_____

_____

Honor Yourself. I acknowledge that I am doing well in some areas, and I agree to continually educate and improve myself where needed.

_____   _____

Name   Date

Chapter 4

The IDENTITY Piece

ഇ

"When you become the image of your own
imagination, it's the most powerful
thing you could ever do."
- RuPaul[9] -

Keeping Yourself

The room was full of activity. Hats, coats, shoes, belts, tools, and an assortment of objects flung across the room. There was a rush to find just the perfect item in the pile of treasures. Beads for a necklace, stethoscope for a belt, an old rag for a bandanna—all meticulously placed at the whim of each child. Dress-up time was in fact our kids favorite time of day. What came prancing out of the room was picture worthy—a moment to remember. Each of my three children touted what they believed to be the finest creation. The oldest was decked in a full Spider-Man costume with a face mask peeled back to create a turban. Attached to various parts of his body was an arsenal of weapons beyond what the original character would have worn. This gadget was for cooking, the next was for trapping lions, the third was to tell the time. Our second child donned parts of a child's hospital gown saved from a trip to the ER. The gown was smothered with jackets and sweaters. He layered his outfit to reflect all the things he liked. Several hats were smashed awkwardly on his tiny head giving him the appearance of something from outer space. On his feet were cute fuzzy baby-blue bunny slippers. They looked painfully too small. My third child proudly displayed a fire hat, an earring made from a baby toy, and the left over parts of last year's Buzz Lightyear™ costume. A small pirate patch clung to his forehead drastically impairing his vision.

What struck me was, that even though each of my children was covered in random clothes, their personalities shown loud and clear. No amount of clothing could hide who they were.

The opposite was quite true. Each article of clothing took on the characteristics of the child wearing them. The children's identities were not lost. They were in fact clarified.

Many parents I have talked to often bring up the topic of their loss of identity. This is assuming that they knew who they were before they had children. There seems to be a magic parent costume you can slip on that will automatically transform and transcend the individual wearing the costume. Never is this the case. Parent costumes only drown the individual in an over-stuffed-shell that is supposed to be them but never is. The result is loss of Self and the loss of identity.

My goal through this chapter is to help unzip your parent costume and free you to be the real parent you were meant to be.

How you define yourself is simply a noun; a noun refers to persons, places, things, states, or qualities.[10] You are much more than a label. Labels are helpful for us as a community to quickly sort multiple items. Imagine going into a grocery store and being told that the store was not using labels or signs anymore. "Feel free to browse around," you are told. "We just don't have any labels." I am not here to bash labels. Labels are useful. Labels are, however, shortened abbreviations of the real item.

Unfortunately, many of us have allowed nouns to define our authentic Self. We have allowed nouns to become our **exclusive** identity.

I am "a **manager**."

I am "a **black** person."

I am "a **white** person."

I am "a **Christian**."

I am "an **Atheist**."

I am "a **city** person."

I am "a **country** person."

I am "a **husband**."

I am "a **wife**."

I am "a **parent**."

Doesn't this short list of labels bore you just reading it? Our first introductions of ourselves are often a laundry list of all the things we do. And many times we choose to be defined by this list. While I am not here to lecture you on the dangers of label identities, I am here to help you get out from behind one label—that of PARENT.

I want you to free yourself from the definition of a parent. Listen carefully to what I said. I did not say quit being a parent. I said you are **more** than a parent. What we do as a profession or passion is only part of who we are as a person. In fact, it is never **who** we are but an **expression** of who we are.

I have seen parents fall into depression and desperation simply because they have self-identified as **only** a parent. Oh, it may be cute in the beginning if you are fortunate enough to have a community around you celebrating your entrance into parenthood. We throw parties and exchange gifts to show how delighted we are with this new phase of life—and rightly so. But then the parties end, and the work begins. The separation and reality sets in. Loss of sleep, loss of friends, and loss of free time are usually not on anyone's bucket list. Often times, it is hard to see beyond the physical moment of changing diapers and fixing bruised knees. We look in the mirror and can wonder where we went? Where did this young vibrant individual disappear to? You know that you are more than the activities of being a parent. You are more than what you do.

You can see that knowing what pieces make you unique and the ability to place these pieces in a way to make a beautiful work of art is a process that starts before and goes well beyond the scope of parenting. The first work we need to do is understand who we are without nouns, external thoughts, or opinions of others. We need to strip off all the dress-up clothes, and get down to the basics of us. You have started this process through the first several chapters of this book. I am challenging you to keep taking off anything that doesn't resonate as yours. Let it drop off. You are safe.

I want to be clear that I am not asking you to permanently leave every external idea or every influential person on the floor. I am not asking you to neglect your responsibilities. All these ideas and experiences are right where you left them—if and when you need them. I am asking you to put them aside for now, and allow yourself to see YOU. You are wonderful and powerful. You are an awe-inspiring creature. Everything leading up to this point has led you here. You are perfectly where you were meant to be. Often it is life experiences that help guide us and gives us the knowledge of what works and what does not work. Life has brought you here. Be thankful for that. I am not asking you to leave your life. I am wanting your life to reflect you. I am asking you to be brave. Do not be afraid of life. Learn from life.

You are going to do things that you think back about later and ask yourself, "What was I thinking?" You, as a parent, have fit the wrong "piece" of you into the wrong "place" of parenthood many times. It happens. The question is what are you going to do about it? Are you going to leave it where you know it does not belong? Or are you willing to see the piece, own the piece, and rearrange the pieces over and over again until you find a place that fits? Are you willing to remove a "piece" that you know is not yours and trust that you will find a "piece" that fits? I know you can.

Allowing Yourself To See

Becoming a parent is a very eye-opening process. From the moment I and my husband made the decision to add children into the family structure, it has been a change like none other. Parenting children, unlike a lot of other types of parenting, really brings to light who you are. Kids have a gift for exposing all of our character traits, our beliefs, and our true intentions.

In our social interactions and through social media, my husband and I have been pretty forthcoming with information, pictures, and details in regards to our children. One thing I have come to learn about sharing our children in the community and on the internet is that it always elicits a response and an emotion. This can be good or bad, but people do pay attention when it comes to kids. There is something about children that touches the hearts of most people. I believe children affect us for many reasons. For starters, we were all children at one time. So, for some people, when they see a parent/child interaction, it reminds them of their past. For others, this interaction is a mirror and/or motivator for their own parenting. And for others, it is an image of how they want their future family to be.

So, as I began to share more about our children, things became clearer. Honestly, it really was not as much about the sharing of our children as it was about the vulnerability to voice who I was and what I was doing. And through that vulnerability, I was finding out a lot about myself. I realized that, probably for the first time, people really saw who I was. I was seeing who I really was. I did not have all the answers. I had a lot to figure out. However, I realized that life is not about having the complete or perfect picture. Life is about honoring the pieces you do have and learning how to put the pieces together.

Yes, other people help bring focus to your life. This is the benefit of having a community, no matter how distant, disturbed, displaced, or even dysfunctional. Sometimes, we do not see ourselves for who we really are and what we bring to the table. We also do not see the opportunity to grow and change until faced with an external opinion and observation that informs us otherwise. This is where your past has helped you. However, now it is time to allow yourself to see YOU.

PARENTING WITH PIECES

The question of who you are is daunting to most. On the surface, this question seems harmless but (like an iceberg) its power lies in the things we do not see. Who we are is not always as clear and simple for us adults. No matter what answer you give to the question, it seems to be lacking. How do you fit all of who you are into a label or even a sentence? Any answer will always pale in comparison to the shining splendor that is You. You are more than what has defined you or even how you have defined yourself.

You simply are.

We have heard the old clichés such as "Don't die a copy when you were born an original" or "Be you, because everyone else is taken." Any time you define something, you restrict its potential and power. When you drop the definers, all that is left is—I AM.

Remember the points in your life where you felt most alive. What were the elements that made up those experiences? What were the pieces? What were you good at? What made you full of energy? Think of any moment big or small. Somewhere inside that experience is your identity. The real you. The reason why you felt the way you did is because you were operating as your true Self. I am not talking about the activities themselves. I am talking about what made you sparkle as you were doing those activities. You can have that kind of inspired living even as a parent. Actually, this is the kind of living that will cause you to be a great parent. Your family wants you—The Real You.

The IDENTITY Piece

Writing a book, especially one that is focused on helping others improve their lives was an undertaking that I took seriously. Just getting to the point of narrowing down what I wanted to write about (and could write about) was half the battle. The other half was believing in myself enough to actually start writing. Though I have always wanted to write, it was not until 2010 that I initiated the process and 2015 when I actively settled on what I was to write about. Yes, it took five years just to have enough clarity and vision to see through the fog.

I have always been a communicator personally and professionally; verbally that is. I could speak. I could teach and speak for hours at a time. That was easy to me. However, communicating verbally and communicating through the written word required different skill sets altogether. I was stuck. Not because I lacked having things to say but because every time I put the words to paper they reflected back to me who I was in a way that I had never faced before. I did not know if I liked what I saw. I did not know if I agreed with what I saw. I did not know if what I saw was really me. I had words to say, but were these the words I wanted to say? Really, I was asking who am I? I was asking who do I want to be, and who do I want the world to see? I knew I had to be authentic. This was the only way for me to write. And if I was not comfortable with the image I saw reflecting back at me, then I needed to work on me until I found something I liked or until I found out who the real me was. Five years later, I had a reflection that I liked and more importantly a reflection that was me.

One of the teachers I admire in philosophy and spirituality is Deepak Chopra who once said, "Every great change is preceded by chaos."[11] In the process of building ourselves and creating a thriving environment, we may encounter things that are seemingly chaotic. Organizing your life is about learning the "who, what, when, where, why, and how" of your life pieces. You are going to start to build your foundation. Building a foundation can be a messy job; just ask any construction worker. There are many similarities to building a foundation for a mansion and building a foundation for your own mindset.

Do you feel like you have known yourself in the past? Then I am just reminding you of the person you are. Realigning yourself and remembering your specific pieces will not be difficult. You have worked within your identity before and this will be a refresher course to allow you to strengthen who you are. But what if you never knew YOU? What if you have been going along trying to define yourself by what everyone else wants or what everyone else thinks? What do you do? You go through this process. You are not late or behind. You are ready.

Don't rush through this step. Come back to this step as needed. Taking the time to really "know thyself" is a critical ingredient to parental (or any) success and sustainability. Who we are is a collective entity of our past, our principles, our privilege, our pain, our ideology, and pathology. So let's find out who you are.

Who are you? If you don't have children ...
Who are you? Apart from your children ...

Who are you? If you never get married …
Who are you? Apart from your partner(s) …
Who are you? In your current career …

Who are you?

Never Despise Small Beginnings

Again, every **thing** and every **thought** has a beginning—a place in which it originates. Something new is beginning in you, right now, as you are reading this book. This is life changing and this change brings life. As you start this process of creating more favorable experiences in your life, we must start with words; words that you tell yourself and words that are being told to you. Words always create the world in which we live; internally and externally. Words create a picture of how we view ourselves, others, and our options in the world. I want you to do three things.

Find your own words. **Use** your own words. **Own** your own words.

You do not have to have a lot of words. It is ok to start small, especially if you have been used to hearing external sources. Be kind to yourself. Keep trying. Keep listening. Enjoy the voice that is inside you and encourage it even if it is small. Remember, never despise small beginnings.

One of the great British politicians, Benjamin Disraeli, once said, "Change is inevitable. Change is constant."[12] Later the popular American speaker John C. Maxwell stated that "Change is inevitable, but growth is optional."[13] I am going to adjust these quotes for our purposes and say that **"Change is inevitable and Growth is intentional."**

Change is arguably the only constant in life. All things change. However, all things do not grow. All things do not develop. All things do not progress. Yes, change is inevitable. But is your change toward your development or your decay? This is solely up to you. You have the right, the responsibility, and the reward of taking charge of your life and writing or rewriting your story. You do this by rearrange the pieces of your life to make them work in your favor! But, I want you to not only change but also grow. I want you to develop in your growth. I want you to progress in your growth! I want you to learn to be intentional. I want you to be an active participant in the process because change is a built-in and automatic function of life.

You may say, "Change is scary!" I know. I understand. The reason why change is so scary is that it usually involves adjusting your thoughts of your identity. Let me assure you that the change we are talking about is not changing you or your identity. Quite the opposite. The change I am talking about is the change that allows your true identity to come forward.

Yes, we want things to change. But wanting something to change and knowing how to make it change are different things altogether. I have said before we must first change ourselves before expecting a situation to change. And while you can change your external experiences through your internal experience, your goal is never just the outward experience. Why is this? When you change one external situation, another external situation replaces it. This process is recurring. External events are temporal. They shift into a new event. However, when you change yourself internally—it is so. You have changed. You will not change until the next decision has been made by you to change you. You are the constant. You are irreplaceable. This change becomes sustainable. This change is eternal.

So, how can you change and grow intentionally? Growing, developing, and changing intentionally means that you are not waiting for something else or someone else to do anything. You begin to realize that you have power over your life and your life is not simply happening **to** you but happening **through** you, **with** you, and more importantly **for** you. You affect life and not the other way around. So, living intentionally really starts with you changing your perception. Max Planck, a German theoretical physicist, once said "When you change the way you look at things, the things you look at change."[14] Dr. Wayne Dyer, who is one of my favorite philosophers and teachers, has often quoted this very saying.[15]

So true.

A changed life begins with the willingness to change and the courage to continue changing. Since you are reading this book, I know you are seeking change and answers. Changing your internal conflicts does not mean changing your identity. And, changing your external circumstances does not mean you have to lose everything environmentally valuable. I know I keep repeating this point, but it is important to hear. Change is simply the courage to perceive what **is** and place it in its **most effective** position. It is about putting the piece in the most desired spot. Notice, I did not say putting the piece in the "right" spot. There is no "right" spot, and consequently, there is no "wrong" spot either.

Everything simply is.

So, how did I do it? There are many ingredients as I have alluded to but four stand out to me.

First, acknowledge what other people are saying are your strengths and weaknesses.
Second, be bold enough to say I have those strengths.
Third, be brave enough to say, I have those weaknesses.
Fourth, begin the work.

Acknowledging what other people are saying about you is often the hardest but the most rewarding. Really listening to what people are saying about us and not just listening to what we want to hear is an eye-opening process. Yes, you are correct—this is external. Most of us do not take the challenge of listening. We do not listen because truth, at times, can be brutal. We love hearing the positive things about us more than we do the negative. We give ourselves excuses if someone reflects to us a part of us that is rough around the edges. But we always know the truth.

There are two detrimental responses to listening to the truth. One response is to absorb all the negative reflections we see about ourselves and spiral into despair and self-mutilation. The other response is to focus only on the positive reflections and puff ourselves up bigger than a blimp. Either response develops a skewed and stunted version of our true Self. The healthy response is to work with all truth in a balanced way. So what do we do once we know the truth?

First, how do we deal with "negative" attributes of our personality or character? Well, let me point out—they are not really negative. What we label as negative is simply an attribute or solution mismatched with an answer. Another way to say this is you have one of your pieces in the wrong place.

Take a thief for example. While society at large would consider thievery a negative attribute, the skill set to be an effective crook can be somewhat impressive. How so? What does it take to be a thief? Well first, I would say a good thief is a problem solver. S/he looks at a situation and dissects all the moving parts, personalities, and opportunities. Thieves understand structural incongruences. They are master manipulators, actors, and story tellers. They possess speed and agility. These same character traits or abilities placed inside a corporate environment would rocket them to financial stardom. Placed inside a theatre, they would be famous for creating renowned characters. Placed inside the sports arena, they would create Olympic athletes like none other. The only difference is where and how the skill-set is used. Helping rearrange their pieces turns a thief into an entrepreneur, Grammy winner, or gold medalist.

Likewise, the "good" parts of ourselves are simply the pieces for which we have already found the perfect space in the puzzle that is our lives. When we can look at both the negative and positive facts of who we are without running from them, then we can start to choose which pieces best fit in what space.

So, after you acknowledge what other people are saying are your strengths and weaknesses you want to be bold enough to say "I am good at _____." In other words, you want to own the parts that are yours. You say, "This is my piece. I am placing myself here." You have already had to start this process in the first step, but now you are taking it public and declaring You to the world. This can be very scary. What if you are wrong? What if this You changes? What if you have to shift your piece to another space? You will only know these answers if you are willing and bold enough to say "I am good at _____ and here is the space I am going to fit."

And while all the above sounds overly simplified, (and it is) the truth of the matter is that even if we have found our way through the first two steps, we sometimes find ourselves frozen like a child first attempting a jump off the high-dive. Those of you who know what I am talking about will understand both the fear and excitement held in that moment of choice. Do I jump or do I stand still? Do I jump or do I climb down the ladder? You have to begin at some point. Oftentimes, you just have to jump.

Chapter 4: The IDENTITY Piece
Placing The Pieces

Based upon this chapter:

1: What makes you full of energy?

_____

_____

2: What makes you really happy?

_____

_____

3: What labels do you have over you?

_____

_____

4: Who are you without those labels?

_____

_____

Who are you? If you don't have children ...
Who are you? Apart from your children ...
Who are you? If you never get married ...
Who are you? Apart from your partner(s) ...
Who are you? In your current career ...

5:   Are there labels you want to get rid of? If so, what are they?

_____

_____

6:   Is your environment conducive for growth?

_____

_____

7:   How is your environment supporting you?

_____

_____

8:   What would you change about your environment?

_____

_____

9:   What do other people say are your strengths?

_____

_____

10:   Do you agree with them?

_____

_____

11: What are you doing to build your strengths?

_____

_____

12: What words do you want to use to describe you?

_____

_____

Honor Yourself. I acknowledge that I am doing well in some areas, and I agree to continually educate and improve myself where needed.

_____   _____

Name   Date

Chapter 5

The STRESS Piece

ॐ

"In times of stress, the best thing we can do for each
other is to listen with our ears and our hearts
and to be assured that our questions are
just as important as our answers."
- Fred "Mister" Rogers[16] -

Safe Seeking Answers

For those individuals within a certain age range, I am sure you remember the half-hour children's television series called *Mister Rogers' Neighborhood*, which was hosted by the hospitable and genuine Mr. Rogers himself. Even more memorable was the opening theme song. "It's a beautiful day in this neighborhood, a beautiful day for a neighbor. Would you be mine? Could you be mine? ... Please won't you be my neighbor?" This song was not just an invitation to enter into a happiness-filled fantasy world. This song was also an invitation to escape the reality of a world of problems, confusion and stress.

Mister Rogers' Neighborhood was in production from 1968 to 1976 and again from 1979 to 2001.[17] The show was aimed primarily at preschool aged children from two to five, however, it had a calm and hypnotizing effect for people of all ages. If you have never seen an episode of *Mister Rogers' Neighborhood*, you are missing out on all the fun. Whether you are a long time "neighbor," or you are just now learning about Mister Rogers, I highly recommend searching online to view some of these classic shows. You will not be disappointed.

The Public Broadcasting Service (PBS) states the summary of *Mister Rogers' Neighborhood* beautifully by saying, "While some adults wonder what makes this television program so fascinating, the children know: Mister Rogers brings them a one-to-one affirmation of their self-worth and offers them a place where they feel accepted and understood."[18]

I believe the true magic of this show did not lie in the fantasy-driven world of children, but in the truthful principles that it revealed to parents. There is something to be said about keeping things simple. As a situation becomes simpler; answers become clearer. When we experience stress, it is often because we overcomplicate a very simple matter.

No matter what you were going through in your day, *Mister Rodgers' Neighborhood*, in the span of that thirty-minute show, could help momentarily shift your focus from stress to serenity. Words like serenity, calm, clear, and simple are not used to describe parents very often.

So how did Mister Rodgers ease our stress? I believe he achieved calm by asking safe questions.

Asking questions is an art. Applying answers is a discipline. Many times we ask questions so we feel better about ourselves and our decisions, but not really to make substantial and sustainable change. We actually can ask questions that trigger stress instead of helping us deal with stress. Questions that trigger stress are unsafe.

How do you ask questions? When we perceive life as providing more questions than answers, we see questions as a sign of insufficiency. Do you know what questions really are? Questions are answers in the process of being discovered. Questions are what we experience when answers seek to call us to a higher level of knowing. This higher level is for ourselves first and then for others second.

I want you to start seeing questions as a quest rather than a conquest—a journey rather than a fight. Parenting is a journey that has many paths and the more eager you are to learn, the more enjoyable it will be. When you view parenting like a conquest, you train your mind to be unconsciously prepared for battle. You are preparing for a fight in which you must win or be defeated. After all, battling is at the heart of every conquest. Both quest and conquest are seeking to obtain something. The difference is that conquest is more about force and quest is more about seeking.

With that being said, we must shift our thinking to be assured that questions are just as important as answers. We want to make sure the questions lead us to solutions. We must begin asking the questions that really matter rather than gauging the next fight. Ask questions that bring about understanding, rather than more mental upheaval.

Let us begin by understanding and answering our first question.

What is stress?

What Is Stress?

Everyone experiences some form of stress. I want to establish this now, so we can remove any barriers or excuses. Your stress is not increased or decreased because of your situation. Redirect your mind from those external thoughts and work internally with me. Yes, you will undoubtedly face various stresses in your life. You may actually start to feel stressed as we talk about stress. This is ok, and you will soon figure out why this is happening.

So, what exactly is stress?

Stress, according to dictionary.com, is "any response that disturbs or interferes with the normal physiological equilibrium of an organism." Also, stress is a pressure or force exerted on one thing by another.[19] We can also describe stress as the importance attached to a thing or emphasis on a thing. I am actually going to use all three definitions because I think they work well together.

Here is an example. You are at home working at your desk. You have importance attached to your work. You have deadlines, goals, and desires all wrapped up in the activities you are engaged in while sitting at your desk. We will assume, for this example, that you love all the work you are doing and are completely fulfilled. You are happy. You are at ease as you continue your work. There is no stress. There is no force pushing against you. There is no disturbance. There is no reaction.

Then, the neighbor's dog starts barking. You love animals but this particular dog seems to know how to get under your skin. Your neighbors seem to be oblivious to the confrontational relationship between their dog and your peace of mind. Every time you try to work at your desk their confounded dog starts barking. You feel your blood pressure rise. You actually start to sweat. Now you have a headache.

What is happening?

You are simply responding to a disturbance or interference—the dog. You are protecting the thing you are attached to or see valuable—your work. Since your concentration is needed to work, and your concentration is pulled to the sound of the dog, you view this dog as exerting force against your work. You view the dog as attacking your work thus attacking you. The one thing that stands in the way of you and the success of your work is that dog! Your stress will signal possible "danger" from the dog. Your stress turns to pain if you choose to continue working. You have that headache. You may not go as far as to say that the dog is your enemy but this is how your body's internal system is responding. This is your true view in this moment. That same dog making the same sounds (but placed in a situation where the dog is not threatening anything you hold valuable) would either be met with apathy and indifference or actual pleasure.

Pain is the next step after stress. When we experience physical pain, it is an indication that something in our body is out of balance or not operating normally. Stress is a first signal. Often, we are not fully aware of our discomfort so pain, in essence, becomes the voice of stress. Anytime you become aware of something, it has been given voice. Pain speaks to us by letting us know that something needs to change. Pain asks us are we willing to change. This pain is an indicator of dis-ease. Pain points you in the direction of that which needs your attention.

The indicator of pain is a personal call to reprioritize your life. Pain seeks a place of balance, order, and peace. While you must acknowledge this pain, you must also learn to view the pain as an ally for your success and not an enemy of your progress. Many of us have been taught that pain is a bad thing and something to be avoided. Pain, like change, is a process of life. For the progressive person, pain is a tool to help clarify what is needed to help move life along. For the passive or problem-focused person, pain is used as a reason to remain a victim to circumstances and an excuse of why things are not changing.

People experience more pain because they are unwilling to intentionally be aware of their own being. Pain then has to step in to be the voice that gets their attention. Our goal is to step in before pain has to do the work for us. Again, pain is not our enemy, but we all recognize that pain is not comfortable. Why choose the path that is more uncomfortable when we could choose an easier approach?

So are we supposed to enjoy and except pain? No, this is not what I am saying. I want you to eliminate the need for pain by learn to bring awareness to yourself. View pain as training wheels on a bike. Pain is there to keep us upright while riding. Once we are better at balancing ourselves on our own "bike," we will not need pain to keep us balanced. This does not mean we will never lose our balance and experience pain again, but we do want to be growing in our balancing abilities. Thoughtful practice and intentional consistent patience will allow us to hear what our bodies need.

Parenting **can** be a stressful, painful process. However, you do not have to accept this as part of the path. The fastest way to get rid of pain is by finding the root cause of the pain. This is what the pain wants you to do anyway. Pain never was intended to **become** your normal. Pain is here to get you **back** to your normal. This is why it is so important to first identify what your true healthy normal is. What is the normal of You or who are You? This is important because your body's system needs to know.

Pain can allow you to feel a myriad of emotions. These emotions, as paralyzing as they may feel, should not stop you from continuing to grow as a person. Learn to shift your thinking about pain. Pain is not a sign that you are somehow wrong, lacking, or deficient. It is a sign that you have one of your pieces in the wrong place. Sometimes, parents are their own worse critics, and they feel guilty if they experience pain. You are not wrong or guilty. All you are doing is allowing pieces to be mismatched. Sometimes we allow our children to place our pieces for us. Sometimes we allow a partner or grandparent or community member to do the placing for us. However well-intended these people may be, they will never be able to perfectly match our pieces in the right places. I do not advocate we remain in stressful and painful situations. I am recommending that each of us see pain as a teacher. This teacher is inside everyone. When we see pain as a teacher, we can position our thinking into one of inquiry rather than intimidation.

One thing I have found helpful when dealing with pain is to again ask safe questions. I have learned to talk and listen to the pain directly through the process of questioning. Think of this as a form of self-therapy.

Ask pain;
What am I feeling?
Pain, what does this mean?
What should I do?
What do you want me to notice?
Is this the first time I have felt you?
Pain, why have you returned?
What did I do to fix this last time?
How did I get out of balance again to allow this you to show up?

A force-focused parent looks to get rid of all pain. This person confronts pain like they are on a demolition site. Pain must be destroyed.

A seeking-focused parent finds ways to understand why pain is present. They become their own investigator and their own physician. They learn to become skilled in the art of recognizing the causes and symptoms of pain. They work on providing their own remedies for pain.

But why, for some of us, is pain such an active part of our life? Why does it seem to be an old friend? I believe the answer lies in the beginning.

From Pleasure To Pain

Alex looks at his watch. He has been planning this event ever since he set eyes on Rachel. Has he done everything on his list? He checks one more time. Flowers—check. Dinner reservations—check. Clean and matching outfit—check. Cologne—check. All seems to be ready. His heart races in anticipation. Everything must be perfect.

Fast forward and Rachel is waiting. What will the answer be? They have hoped for this moment for years. Ever since their first date she knew Alex was the one. Yes, his clothes were a little mismatched, and she was allergic to the flowers he gave her—she did not care. She loved their first date, and she loved him. How thrilled she was that he asked her out again and again. Weeks turned into months, and their hearts and minds intertwined. Life was so good. Then it got better. Alex said, "Will you …?" and Rachel said, "I do!" Rachel sits on the bathroom counter thinking about their history. She waits. Then the answer comes! They are having a baby!

Immediately life changes. The joy, the anticipation, the hopes, the plans. Rachel thinks about their future. What will the child look like? Who will the child favor? Who will the child act like? She plans.

The STRESS Piece

Our child will have his eyes and my nose. Or maybe the other way around. I bet the child walks like him. S/he will definitely have my hair. Oh, I hope our child is perfect. S/he will be perfect.

Rachel and Alex begin making changes that are in the best interests for their child. They begin constructing an environment—an Eden—where this child has all of its needs met and many of his wants as well. This paradise would be filled with all the best. Rachel eats differently and acts differently. She wants this baby to have the best from the very beginning. She feels herself change and grow. She grows mentally, spiritually, and of course physically.

For months everyone works toward the birth of the child. Even the child is working. The baby works on growing into a more defined form. Alex and Rachel educate themselves on how to be effective parents. Rachel consults with her doctor on the progress of her body and the baby. The parents are child-focused. The child is growth-focused.

The first thing prepared for the child is the environment. The womb is designed to keep the child physically safe, give nutritional sustenance, and provide the first model of how life should really be. The ears are one of the first external physical features that develop. The child faintly hears something. The sound is consistent in its rhythmic expression. Thud! Thud! Thud! The sound mixes with a feeling. The child feels the sound of its own heart. The child's hearing gets stronger as the days progress and now the child can hear what sounds like the rushing waves of the sea. This is the water-like environment of the womb itself.

Moment by moment and day by day, the child's hearing grows to hear something new. It sounds just like the child's heartbeat but it's different. This is the sound of Rachel's heartbeat. Sometimes the beats are in sync and sometimes slightly off. Either way, the sound is always there. The sound of the waves are carrying the beats back and forth, like a conductor leading an orchestra. This trinity of noise sounds like a song. A song that never stops and never fades away. This other sound is the first clue that the child is not alone.

I am sure you are imagining yourself as the child experiencing all of this in the womb and how great it is. It is safe. It is fun. It is exciting! You have the freedom of exploration. You have safety and comfort. How does it feel knowing that you are so cared for and so loved?

Since you are already imagining yourself as the child, I want you to see yourself in the womb. See yourself as you sway back and forth as you hear the gentle sounds all around you. The weeks progress and you have developed your eyes, hands, fingers, legs, and toes.

You begin to have the ability to be more aware of yourself and your surroundings. You get a hint that you have developed something new. You will soon know them as your eyes. While your eyelids are still closed, you can sense light outside the womb. You can move your eyes back and forth. Now you accidentally learn how to open your eyes. You begin to get that sensing again, that feeling of light, and this time you not only look but you start to move. Oh wait, you also have feet! You have hands! Your feet and hands all move in concert with your eyes as you respond to the light.

Your hearing is much stronger now. You hear people giggling. You get a rush of emotions. You start to feel happiness, joy, safety, and belonging. You hear a voice say, "The baby just kicked!" and another voice respond with, "Wow!" as awed hands gently rest on your outer sanctuary.

For weeks, this nurture continues. The home that once was spacious, now has the feeling of limitation and confinement. You are stronger now. You try to move more but feel the resistance of your environment. You push, and your environment feels like it is pushing back in opposition.

You take a while, possibly days, to reflect upon what has happened and what this means for your future. Your feelings of excitement and joy transform into worry and frustration. Even though these emotions feel like yours—they also feel foreign, like you are feeling what someone else is feeling. You no longer feel safe. You feel like an intruder.

You continue to think.

Until …

Something is starting to happen.

There is a lot of movement. You feel both excited and nervous as vibrations get faster and harder. You are hearing screams, instructions, crying, and shouts. Now you feel like someone is forcefully pushing you somewhere. There are bright lights and a strange feeling on your skin. You are not where you have been and the shock to your system registers as painful. This is not your normal way of being. Pain says something is wrong. You cry!

Welcome to a whole new world.

Let us take this moment and reflect. What have you gone through? Think about the entire journey from start to now, and reflect on how you are feeling physically and emotionally. Yet, the journey is only beginning.

As we think back on the child, we all know what is occurring.

With many cries the mother pushes her child from the comfort of it's womb into the seeming chaos of this world. The child is forced, by nature and by humanity, to leave what has been familiar and go to what is new. And this newness triggered stress which was voiced by pain. Pain was saying go back to our normal, our balance, our peace. Go back to the womb. The child went from a place of pleasure to one of pain.

Replacing The Pain

So, thus far we understand that all pain is a response to stress and is a voice drawing our awareness to something our bodies seem to think is a problem. We understand that pain is neither good nor bad, but is a tool to help us navigate and thrive. Now the question is, what do we do with pain? I first need to make a distinction between two types of pain before I can answer that question. I will identify the two types of pain as systematic pain and growing pain.

When I speak of our "system," I am talking about everything that is us. I am referring to all that is physical, mental, emotional, and spiritual. Systematic pain shows up when our system detects something that, to us, is out of our normal—something our system sees as sabotaging our well-being. Take for example that back pain in the morning. Your body is saying you slept wrong during the night or the bed is not suited to you getting a good night's rest. "Please change our sleeping arrangements in the future!" pain says. Or imagine you stub your toe or bang your head on a freshly cleaned sliding glass window—as I once did. Pain would say, "This activity of banging one's head into glass is not good for our body or wellbeing. Please stop!" So we make arrangements to do what pain tells us to do. We use caution the next time we come across the same door. We double check to see if the glass door is opened or just really, really clean. We do whatever it takes to balance out our world so we can get back to the business of harmonious growth and peaceful balance. We are trying to get back to our normal. We do this without having to be told. We do this automatically. What a wonderful system we have.

The second kind of pain is growing pain. We actually know this pain from our physical bodies growing. My husband, as a teen, went through a growth spurt as most teenagers tend to do. He tells the story of how the week before he was going to summer camp he had such pain in his lower back that he could not walk or move. Finally, he saw a chiropractor and my husband's back was adjusted. One leg had grown faster than the other leg, and this pinched a major nerve in his back. Once he got the adjustment he could stand, walk, and play with no pain. His body had shifted into his new normal; which in this case was a bigger physical body.

I used two examples of physical pain, but the same principles apply to our mental, emotional, and spiritual parts as well. So, pain is pain. Although pain may try to tell you what to do about the situation, it really is not the job of pain. Remember pain is the voice saying something is "wrong." This is where you, as the controller of your own being, come into play. You are the puzzle master. You are the one who needs to tell you what is going on and what you are going to do about it. You need to know You thoroughly. Then you will understand the situation truthfully. You need to make knowledgeable and safe decisions for you to balance, expand, or do both. You actually need to be your own parent.

The interesting thing is that pain does not know the difference between something that is good for you (growth) and something that is harmful to you (banging your head into the glass). Pain just says "STOP THIS!" Pain is never interested in growth but is interested only in returning you to what has been the standard experience. Pain wants you to be back to "normal."

Go back to the baby being born in our previous example. The act of being birthed puts stress on the baby's system and therefore registers as pain. The pain is not wrong. The pain says "Something is changing—our normal is shifting. We do not like this change." What the pain does not understand is that while the womb seems very safe at the moment, staying inside the womb forever will actually result in death.

Pain wants it both ways. The system (or baby) sensed that something was going on and pain (if you will) was complaining when the baby did not have enough room to move about. Again pain said, "Something is changing. We seem to be getting bigger, or our house (our Eden) is getting smaller. We used to have so much more room. Give us back our big environment." Now that the baby has been born and has much more room, pain says, "Wait! What happened to the womb? This is big and different. We want the womb back!" All pain is doing is trying to keep our system operating as usual. Pain is doing its job.

So, what do we do? Now you can see why I am big on asking questions. Depends. What is going on? Where do we want to go? Are we growing? If we are, then by definition we are asking for our normal to change. We will have some level of "pain" only because our system is going to want to resist that change until it gets used to it. Ask any athlete, artist, business person, or any successful individual what it took to become who they are. You will find that they all started out as someone very different than who they are now. They changed. They grew. And that growth always brought about a level of discomfort or pain.

However, if our system is under attack; if we are in danger, then we need to take quick and sure measures to get our systems back on track. We need to fix the problems so we can thrive again. We should listen to pain. Running will fix the problem of being eaten by a predator. Paying attention to glass doors will keep our skulls from being bruised and our brain will thank us.

Once we know what we are dealing with; once we have decoded the message pain is giving us; once we clearly understand where we are going, then we can give commands. When we know we are growing, we can tell ourselves that we will get used to this in time. When we are threatened, we can remove the threat, or remove ourselves from the threat. We can stop and fix the problem. We want to respond (or act) and not just react. We can now replace the pain with actionable steps to take us where we need to go. We can shift our pain's perspective on what is going on. We can arrange the pain piece and place it in a different spot of our puzzle where it no longer registers as a threat.

Learning From Animals

I need to stop here for a moment and address something that often happens between the point stress enters our body and the moment we are aware of pain.

Think about the gazelle being chased by a lion. What would happen to the gazelle if it waited to feel pain before it took action? We all know the answer to that. Many times our system goes on automatic responses before we have a chance to "think" about what is going on. This is great. You do not want to think about breathing every time you have to take a breath. You want your system to do things on its own to protect and keep you safe. This way you can focus on more important things like thriving.

So, many times before we can even experience pain, our system steps in as a response to stress. The three most common responses to stress are fight, flight, or freeze. The fight-flight-freeze response is a biological response of humans and other animals to an acute or sudden stress.

Physiologist Walter Bradford Cannon states that animals react to threats with a general discharge of the sympathetic nervous system, priming the animal for fighting or fleeing. The sympathetic nervous system originates in the spinal cord and its main function is to activate the physiological changes that occur during the fight or flight response. Examples of physiological changes are:

- heart rate and blood pressure increases
- digestive processes slow
- adrenaline and cortisol increases
- sweating increases
- muscles tense

The term sympathetic nervous system was first used medically by Galen, a Greek physician.[20] It can be traced to the concept of sympathy, in the sense of "connection between parts." The term was later applied to nerves. Our system "feels" sympathetic to our well-being and jumps in to help. Look at these three ways our system steps in before we can even feel pain.

When we fight:

This is when we push back in the face of danger. We feel we can take the danger head on. We do this when we have experienced this particular danger before and we are seeking to "stand our ground."

When we take flight:

This is when we run and evade danger and try to escape. When we feel that we cannot escape the danger, then we usually turn to flight.

When we freeze:

When we feel overpowered or overwhelmed by the potential threat, we stop and are often in a state of shock until the threat subsides.

The threats we feel internally cause us to have external responses. Our responses to fight, flight, or freeze can occur due to an actual or perceived event that is harmful or that threatens our survival. The mind does not distinguish between "reality" and "fantasy." Sometimes we feel stressed even when there is no immediate cause for us to be stressed. And when the mind perceives a threat, our entire body seeks to protect itself. This primitive response, specifically fight and flight, actually infuses us with strength, power, and speed to avoid the potential harm.[21]

All parents experience moments of pain but not all parents are paralyzed by it. You are not alone in the pain you are feeling. It does not matter whether the pain is physical, emotional, spiritual, financial, relational, or otherwise. We all have pains we experience. Pain can take many shapes, and the shapes change from person to person. What one person calls unbearable pain, is another's "not so bad" pain, or "I'll get over it soon" pain. What is one person's "level 8" pain, may be someone else's "level 5." What makes one person pass out from pain, may make someone else just uncomfortable. As humans, both male and female, we have an amazing ability to endure pain. We also have very different tolerances and responses to pain.

There are some similarities among all mammals and some stark differences. The biggest difference between us and wild animals is that we may be too smart for our own good.

In the book, "Waking The Tiger: Healing Trauma", Dr. Peter Levine[22] offers hopeful suggestions for those of us that have experienced stress in our lives. In his studies, Dr. Levine discovered that prey animals in the wild, while experiencing routine threats to their lives, are rarely traumatized.

How do we manage the stress of it all? And why do the animals have a leg up on humanity when it comes to responses to stress?

Paul Chubbuck, of ReleasingThePast.com states,

"Think of an animal in the wild — a rabbit, for example. It may be calmly eating one moment at the edge of a meadow, and running for its life from a wolf the next. Imagine if that happened to you! That would be pretty traumatic, having a hungry animal determined to catch, kill, and eat you! Yet if the rabbit escapes, then within minutes it will be back to normal life, not traumatized.

"Those who have been able to closely observe wild animals notice that during the time immediately following such a chase, a prey animal will "discharge" that powerful "flight-fight" energy by twitching, shaking, jumping, running around vigorously, even making some noise or head-butting some of its own kind in mock-battle. After such discharge, the animal returns to normal.

"Were it not for this ability to rapidly discharge adrenalin and excess survival energy, the animal's ability to meet future threats would be reduced and they would not long survive in the wild. Even though animals in the wild routinely experience life-threatening situations, after the danger has passed, they quickly return to normal, whereas humans sometimes are stuck with trauma or Post Traumatic Stress Disorder (PTSD). In other words, they are stuck in some combination of the nervous system's fight, flight or freeze response.

"It is like having both the accelerator pedal and the brake pedal pressed to the floor at the same time. The person may think they got over the experience, but if they were unable to avoid the danger and didn't have support to shake off the strong charge of sensations and emotions afterward, that vast amount of survival energy can become

stuck in their nervous systems. Weeks, months, or years later, often without even a conscious connection to the traumatic experience, many different kinds of symptoms may appear. Such symptoms are normal for a person with an over-stressed nervous system. They have lost resiliency, the natural ability to flow easily between the many moods and energy states necessary to live a full and rich life."[23]

How many times do you really allow yourself to discharge your negative experiences? Most of us don't. We allow time to march on without rebalancing our system. Maybe you do not have to twitch, shake, or jump like the rabbit, but how are you discharging that physical survival energy? Maybe a run would do you good. Yes, maybe you do need to make some strange noise in the privacy of your room. Maybe your discharge is something subtler. Whatever it is make sure you know what allows you to safely discharge this energy so you can start to rebalance and return to your healthy normal. If you hold survival energy inside you, it will skew your response to normal everyday events. You can become over-stressed which of course will lead to pain.

Whenever we experience pain, trauma can be created. Trauma is another word for injury and is often but not always used when referring to some experience of external physical harm. Sometimes this can be a perceived danger, rather than an actual one. Typically a trauma challenges us at our core need— survival. All things come down to us feeling safe and secure.

Trauma may result from many different stressors such as loss of a job, invasive medical surgery, death of a loved one, emotional abuse, physical or sexual assault, natural disasters, birth complications, ongoing fear, severe conflicts, war, and accidents just to name a few. But can we really create our own trauma?

Repeating The Pain

Think about your life. How many times have you mulled over something "bad" that happened? How many times did you think about it … over and over and over?

Exactly.

We have been taught that thinking like this is typical and even normal. Many have thought this to be healthy, when in fact it may be contributing to your continued stress. We believe that if we think about the experience again that somehow we will resolve it. We think that there will be a different outcome; a possible answer within the chaos. We think we are resolving the situation when in fact we are repeating the situation with no resolution. We are traumatizing ourselves again and again and again. What was external injury has now become internal injury. Every time we think about our traumatic experience, we incorporate it into our "normal." And because our mind does not know the difference between the real event and our rehearsal of it, we have made the problem worse. Oftentimes, we even embellish the events thereby creating a more traumatizing experience than the original event. Again, our system believes us. We can then experience flashbacks, nightmares, and a host of other negative experiences. We actually relive the event physically. This drains our system, uses up valuable resources, and triggers other destructive behaviors.

Children can be a stressor, which can cause trauma in the life of a parent. I know many may think, "How can a child cause trauma? This does not sound right." If you do not have children yet, just wait and you will understand. And no, I am not a bitter parent who resents his children. Regardless of the love you have for your child, you can still experience trauma from your child directly or indirectly. The birthing process in and of itself is stress, pain, and trauma. This trauma is usually resolved or discharged once the healthy and living baby is born, but this experience is a trauma nonetheless.

Children can unintentionally reintroduce us to past stressful situations. This concept may sound odd, but it is a form of what we call complex trauma. This type of stress can be confusing because you love your child on one end, but on other end, you may seek avenues to protect yourself from your child because of the pain. You accumulate not only the stress of your past but also the present stress introduced by the child. Then you may add other stresses that you experience throughout the course of the day. This revolving door of stress can feel like you are being mentally assaulted. How you think in these situations is critical for your sustainability and success with overcoming trauma.

Yes, we have difficulty releasing trauma because we do not discharge, and we think too much about the negative events in our lives. Our trauma becomes rooted deeper in our psychological, philosophical, and physiological framework.

But, you are not a bad person for doing this. All you are doing is trying to protect yourself. Your system does not love or hate anything. It does not hate your child. Your system is looking out for you. And when it senses experiences that it deems unhealthy for you, your system will try to autocorrect itself.

However, your system may not always have the signals correct. This is why you need to know You more than your system does. You want to step in and take your system off autopilot when desired. This gives you healthy ways to manage and release your stress, so that you can thrive personally and as a parent.

Go back to the illustration of when I hit the glass door with my head. What if I continued to bash my head against the clean glass door every time I walked outside? Over time, my system would shift to the new normal of head bashing. Pain's voice would become softer and softer and bashing my head which was once seen as a problem to my system, would now become what is expected—my new normal. Pain would then work in the opposite direction and convince me to continue banging my head. If I ever stopped banging my head on the glass door, pain would say, "Wait, that's not normal. We usually bang our head when we leave the house. Go back and bang your head. Get back to normal. This is what we expect." At this point, if I intentionally or unintentionally let pain be the director of my life, I would continue to damage my head.

I use this humorous example because it is simple to understand. Most of us would agree that battering our skull on glass is not a good idea. But most of us do this all the time without even knowing it. We have allowed pain to take over our lives in a certain area and we have it all backwards. Be careful to use pain the way pain was intended—as a voice not a friend.

So what do we do? Do we just forget things happened? Do we forget our problems? Well, yes and no. I would ask what is the purpose of remembering or replaying our trauma? Are we coming up with actionable lessons? If so, great! But if we are repeating the movie in our head, hoping there will be a different ending, we will continue injuring ourselves.

Having said that, your past is important. Your past is the foundation for your perspectives. It is the lens through which you view everything. What makes the past so powerful are the stories we tell ourselves about our past. Many emotions may flood your mind when thinking about your past—joy, pain, gratefulness, warmth, terror, sadness, hope, and so on. This is a normal process. The past is important to discuss because it gives a window into who you are and why you do what you do. Who you are now is who you have been becoming. What you do now is the summary of what you have been experiencing throughout your journey. How you do something is the result of previous consequences. Rarely does rehearsing a negative past benefit us, but if we know what we are doing, we can use the past to help us resolve matters of the heart, mind, and soul.

I want you to carefully confront your past **not** to **change** it but to **use** it. I know this is a very fine line. How do you know if you are repeating the past or learning from your past? You will know by your actions. If you start to react with fight, flight, or freeze than you are repeating the past. Stop! You are not ready to learn from that part of your experience. Start with something smaller and more manageable. Find a subject that allows you to learn without negative reactions.

So, as we become more mindful of the past and its effects on our life, we learn to master our life more intently. Mastering your life starts with owning your story. You want to learn from your story and not repeat it.

Creating A Safe Environment

Parenting does not have to be a chaotic experience for you. I cannot count how many times I have heard people say, "Kids change EVERYTHING about your life." Often this is said with frustration and as a warning to expecting parents. This comment infuses so much fear that it can cause emotional anxiety and parental paralysis.

Yes, things will change when you are a parent. You want this change. But, you do not actually want everything to change. Ideally, I would like **you** to remain **the constant**. Remember, too much change too fast will result in your system thinking that you are in danger. I am trying to avoid fight-flight-freeze reactions. You will have some pain, but I want that pain to be more of growth than it is of perceived "danger." If everything changes when you have children, this can create a level of fear, anxiety, confusion, and instability for you and especially the child. If children can and do change the dynamic of your environment, then who is really parenting? Is the child leading or are you leading? Notice I did not say controlling. I said leading.

I am sure you answered correctly; YOU ARE LEADING. Or maybe you feel your child is leading and that is part of the problem. You know you should be leading. You are responsible for creating a safe environment for yourself and your child. You deserve the right to not have your whole world turned upside down just because another person came into your environment. Owning your personal power as a parent requires you to create a healthy environment, and that starts with you putting a structure in place that works for you.

"But how is this possible?" you ask. "I have a newborn that is feeding every four hours and waking me up during the night. I am a working parent and my day never seems to end. I am a parent of a toddler that is throwing temper tantrums." Or "I have a teen and I am about to go out of my mind with this headstrong individual."

You are right. None of these situations are without stress. Remember, you first and then others. So how do you create a safe environment for yourself so that you can thrive? Again, I will ask you to ask yourself some questions.

When do I get stressed?
What is said?
What is the event surrounding the stress?

Is there a pattern to the stress?

Have I tried solutions in the past?

Was I consistent in the implementation?

What happened?

Why did the result happen?

Please add your own questions.

So are you stressed talking about all this stress? I hope not. I know you want some answers. What can you do to deal with stress? Is there a magic pill to make all of this go away? Well, I am working on the pill but until then let's make a plan. We know that thinking about or replaying the event does not usually help us. But there are some coping skills and conquering strategies that we can employ to help us weather the storm and end up on safe and solid ground. Used with consistency and balance, we can reprogram our minds to release the damage done to our physical bodies. As we know more about how we respond to stress, we can also learn how to recover from it.

I want you to try this three-step process for helping you recover from stress. The three steps are simple! First, you must Discern Your Feelings; then you need to Define Your Focus; finally just Discharge Your Frustrations.

1: Discern Your Feelings

Discerning your feelings is about discovering how you feel. Most of this book I have asked you to do this. What I have been asking you to do is this first step. Know enough about yourself to understand the feeling(s) that are here with you in this moment. When you feel stressed, I want you to begin the process of discovery. Ask yourself what you are feeling in that moment? Do you feel hurt, upset, sad ...? Whatever the feelings are that you find, I want you to pause and rest in those feelings for a few seconds. Notice them. Notice your body. What are you doing with your body? Feel the response your system has to this stress. Can you feel your heart start beating faster or your face turn red? What are the physical signs that say to you "I am getting ready to protect myself?" You now consciously know where you are. However, thinking about the feelings in your current emotional space will only cause you to maintain those feelings. So now, focus on where you want to be.

2: Define Your Focus

Defining your focus is about setting your intent on where you want to be. It is not about focusing on what is presently happening. Think of how you want to feel. Picture that feeling and hold it. Now that you have where you want to go, you must release yourself from revisiting the trauma. Ask yourself "How do I get where I want to go?" There are always solutions and steps to get what you want. Allow yourself to find one or two things that you can do to get you from where you are to where you want to be. Once you have that, move on to step three in this process.

3: Discharge Your Frustrations

Discharging your frustrations is about releasing the pain you have. You might feel a little emotional tug-of-war. This is normal. Every time you feel yourself pulling back to your former frustrations, remind yourself of your focus. Remind yourself that you are safe. Remind yourself that all is well. Remind yourself that you are moving forward in peace. Find something that refreshes you. Everyone is different. This is where knowing yourself and how you operate will serve you well in creating a safe space for you. What are healthy ways that you can rejuvenate your soul, your mind, and your body? When you find the answers make the space and time to discharge the energies that come from feeling stress.

Repeat this process as often as needed and with every stress you may encounter.

Chapter 5: The STRESS Piece
Placing The Pieces

Based upon this chapter:

1: When do you get most stressed?

_____

_____

2: What are the most common words that stress you?

_____

_____

3: What is a common event surrounding your stress?

_____

_____

4: Is there a pattern to your stress?

_____

_____

5: What happens to your body when you get stressed?

_____

_____

6: How do you respond? (Fight, Flight, Freeze)

_____

_____

7: How would you like to respond?

_____

_____

8: What ideas or thoughts can you use to refocus?

_____

_____

9: What action steps can you create to choose a different outcome?

_____

_____

10: What are you feeling when you are stressed?

_____

_____

11: What could your pain be trying to tell you?

_____

_____

12: What do you want to do with the information pain is giving you?

_____

_____

13: How often does this same pain return?

_____

_____

14: Have you become used to this pain?

_____

_____

15: What specific ways can you positively discharge your frustrations?

_____

_____

Honor Yourself. I acknowledge that I am doing well in some areas, and I agree to continually educate and improve myself where needed.

_____   _____

Name   Date

Chapter 6

The EMOTIONS Piece

ೞ

"Do you imagine the universe is agitated?
Go into the desert at night and look at the stars.
This practice should answer the question."
- Lao Tzu[24] -

Is The Universe Agitated?

I heard whispers down the hall. Two of my boys were playing quietly in their room. They were making "cookie salad with marshmallows." A plastic pizza was already in the oven, and there were different colored "coffees" made from spare toys. I was informed of this when I went to check on them. They were buzzing around the room like serious contenders on Top Chef. I was proud of them. There was peace, order, and calm.

My oldest son was rapidly finishing up his homework in the other room. His sole intent was getting some play time before lights out. He threw his paperwork carelessly on the desk and rushed off to finish a few odds and ends. Scampering back into the living room, he announced his homework accomplishments and requested to play with his brothers. I agreed.

Three minutes after his integration into the play space, I heard shouts and frustrated cries. Clanks and bangs broke the hushed workspace. I walked down the hall and poked my head through the doorway. What was once an imaginary culinary operation, was now a war-torn battlefield with children fleeing for their lives. One look and the responsible party hung his head. He knew the rules about play fighting inside the house. Without a word, he walked out of the room and plopped himself on his bed.

Our emotions are one of the greatest tools we have to connect with others and truly understanding ourselves. Emotions are designed to direct our heart and passions towards the people, projects, and perspectives that we hold dear. Emotions often fluctuate, as they should, among varying environments. Emotions and parenting seem to go hand-in-hand. But as parents we have learned to live in emotionally integrated clutter. We often do not know when one emotion starts and another ends. The "good" emotions weave in and out of the "bad" emotions. After a while, the result seems like an incomprehensible and unceasing noise. This can be very annoying and agitating.

Let me ask you the same question that Lao Tzu once asked, "Do you imagine the universe is agitated?"

I went into the room to check on my exiled son and question him on what had gone "wrong." He was perplexed. He explained that he went into the room to play, and somehow he found himself having to defend his knighthood from his threatening brothers. He seemed to honestly not understand how he (once again) had gotten the short end of the stick. My son could see that yes, maybe he shouldn't have brandished a weapon in the house. Yes, he might have not swung so hard as to topple over the pizzeria. But really, he explained—he didn't do anything. "The room was already pretty wild."

Much of what he was expressing was true for **him**. From his perspective, there was no change or shift in his environment. He was already in a state of "crazy" before he entered the playroom. **He** was nervous, agitated, and in a rush. None of this changed just because he went into a different room or got around different people. He actually changed the environment he went into.

Like my son, do you find yourself agitated? Why? What is causing your agitation? Do you tell yourself that being upset is a part of the human experience? Do you tell yourself that it is ok to be agitated sometimes? Do you want to feel agitated? Do you like the consequences of being agitated? We validate frustration, agitation, and other negative emotions in our life based on unmet expectations and misguided intents. Like my son, whose real intent was to shed excess energy before bed, we go into situations confused about what we are creating. Then we are lost when that creation effects our environment. We are frustrated when our expectations are not met. We blame others. We deflect. We are defeated.

I know sometimes it can feel like the world is out of control. You may feel like you are on a battlefield. I know you can feel justified in your frustrations. I have felt exactly how you have felt and so have many others. But if you build the foundation of your life on emotions, your life is susceptible to constant change without stability. This can leave you victimized and imprisoned by your emotions. Why let this happen to you? You can have a solid foundation from which you can express your emotions. Your life can consistently be full of happiness and peace. However, you must learn how to create an environment where you thrive and your emotions are effectively utilized.

So how do we match up this emotions piece with the rest of our puzzle? First, we need to understand the difference between our thoughts, our emotions, and our feelings.

The Environment of Emotions

The word "feeling" and "emotion" are used interchangeably in our society. While there is a relation between these two words, I want you to understand they are not one-in-the-same. A distinction must be made between feelings and emotions in order to truly understand yourself as a sentient being. A sentient being simply means that as humans we feel, perceive, and experience life through our senses. We have a viewpoint of life based upon the five traditionally recognized methods of perception or sensing: sound, sight, touch, smell, and taste. While these senses collectively create our environment, they are understood through two domains: our feelings and our emotions. So, what exactly is the difference? Emotions are biochemical and feelings are sensory.

Emotions can be measured by monitoring our blood flow, body stance, brain activity, facial expressions, and so on.

Feelings are what we can sense such as sound, sight, touch, smell, and taste.

In her article "Emotions Versus Feelings", clinical psychologist Dr. Cindy Meyer, highlighting the work of USC neuroscientist Antonio D'Amasio, M.D, helps bring some clarity to this subject. She says that emotions and feelings are really, "two sides of the same coin" and "like with coins, what you notice will depend upon where you are looking."[25]

I need to stop at this point for a sidebar. While I am going to be focusing on the five senses I want to acknowledge my belief that there are more than five senses. My purpose here is not to instruct on the extra senses we have. I want to bring up this point because here is where we have the debate of what is a feeling. Feelings, oftentimes seem to merge into thoughts and emotions simply because many in the scientific community (as of yet) do not acknowledge the existence of other senses. So when we actually use a sense outside the five we normally acknowledge, we do not know where to place this sense. We try to say it is a thought or an emotion. We get ourselves very confused because we cannot seem to fit this unidentified experience into a category. I belief that in time we will better scientifically understand more of who we are. And when we have allowed ourselves to expand in our knowledge, we will more comfortably be able to talk about our experiences. So basically, if you get confused during this section no problem— many do. I want you to have a general understanding of how you work. You do not need to be an expert in all these areas. Remember you are perfect right where you are —right here, right now. Relax and let's keep going.

The talk was strictly in secret. No one wanted to tell the dads what was going on. Everyone was ready for bed and sporting the finest in bed time accessories. Teeth were brushed and skin was scrubbed. The curtains were drawn and soft music permeated the house. All was set for the calm of the night. Yet it seemed all was not well. I had the distinct feeling, as I made the rounds to say goodnight to my sons, that something was adrift. My second son had a nervous look on his face. He started pulling at his ear which had always been his sign that he was expecting danger. My oldest son was sweating even though he just got out of the bath. There was a general dis-ease in the room. I asked how they were and they (in unison) said they were fine. Their looks told a different story. I thought for sure I was onto something—so I probed.

How had their day been?
Fine.
Did they have anything they wanted to tell me?
No.
Did they know I loved them?
Yes.

I was not reassured. However, not wanting to push things, I reached down to give them each a hug. My second son grabbed me.

"I'm going to have a good night even if they come."
"Who comes?" I asked.
"I can't say it." Came the reply. I looked at my oldest.
"He's talking about vampires."

I inquired how this knowledge had come into their understanding and I was told by my oldest that the kids at school had been talking about such things. He then in turn told his younger brother and now they were planning for the inevitable midnight attack that was sure to come. I looked at their reddened cheeks and rapid breathing. All the signs were there for a quick flight. I of course did my best to calm them down and assure them of their safety, but in their minds the night was sure to be one of peril and treachery.

The question we often have is a bit of a "which came first" question—the chicken or the egg? And in truth, the answer does not matter. What matters is that we know that there **is** an egg and a chicken. What matters is the purpose they both serve. I want to dissect for us emotions and feelings in a concrete way. In order to do that, I want to add one more element into this discussion. I want to add the element of thought. Thoughts are mental or psychological. Any kind of word, picture, or idea that enters or is created in your mind we can group under thoughts. I want to introduce the idea of thought right now (yes the irony is not lost on me) because so many things flow to and from our thoughts. It is almost impossible to talk about emotions and feelings without including our thoughts. So let's review.

Thoughts are mental or psychological. Thoughts are any kind of word, picture, or idea that enters the mind.

Emotions are biochemical or physiological and can be measured by monitoring our blood flow, body stance, brain activity, and facial expressions.

Feelings are sensory and can be measured by what we hear, see, touch, smell, and taste.

When it came to my boy's facing the danger of vampires we can see how thoughts, emotions, and feelings work together to build an experience for them. The reality of **my** world is that all was safe. There were no threats. The reality of **their** world was danger. This thought of danger had been placed in my oldest son's head. He took that thought as his own and passed it onto his younger brother. His younger brother took the thought as his own. The thoughts were born. From those thoughts the emotions and the feelings started their work. The emotions concentrated on preparing the body for war. My sons' heart rate and blood pressure increased. Their adrenaline and cortisol levels increased. Muscles tensed and physical signs of stress showed up. The sensory system registered the sweat and the tense muscles. These were most likely causing some level of unease and pain. This information was used to confirm to the whole body there was in fact danger. The body then sent multiple messages back to the brain that the body was about to be attacked. The brain then confirmed the new thoughts with the old thought and the truth of vampires deepened. This process is very real and very true to the system or body of the individual. This is why we often have a very hard time "talking down" or interfering with this process once it has begun.

Please note that I, in no way, am saying that this process is bad. On the contrary, I believe this is an excellent example of how our bodies or systems are beautifully engineered to thrive and protect us. We are truly magnificent creatures. Our process of understanding how we work is so we can learn two things. First, when to let our system do its work; secondly, when to override the system.

My hope as a father, in the vampire incident, was to assist my children in overriding their systems. I wanted to reset their systems. I was trying to introduce a thought that might counter act their current thought. I was doing this externally with little to no effect. My goal was for their safety. Interestingly enough, they also wanted safety. We just had two different perspectives and two different ways of trying to achieve the same goal.

Let's do an exercise so we can see how this works.

Remember an event of your past. I want to help you distinguish between your thoughts, emotions, and your feelings. You can pick any event but my suggestion is that you make it a rather fun event. Choose something that startled or scared you. The purpose of this exercise is to track your system. I do not want you to go "too deep." We are only learning about how our system interacts with us. So, I want you to think of the last time you were scared, but I do not want it to be something that was truly traumatic. Pick an event where someone jumped out at you or where you had a slight startle.

I am going to pick one of the times I went on a rollercoaster. I love rollercoasters. Feel free to join me on that journey if you want. Go through this exercise yourself with your own example if you have picked something else. The point is to get yourself into the situation and "see" how you use thoughts, feelings, and emotions.

Picture the last time you were on a roller coaster. Now, think of when you were standing in line for the ride. Which ride was it? How long did you wait? Were you alone? Who did you talk with? As you get closer to the front of the line, see the people who have just pulled into the loading station and remember their faces. Where do you want to sit? Do you sit in the back, the middle, or the very front? Do you have to pay just for this ride, or do you have a day pass? Are you gauging which line you need to enter to get your spot? What is around you? Are there monitors playing something about the ride, or are their animated characters setting up the story? What colors do you see? What are the smells? The line moves. What do you have on? Look at your feet? Where are you standing? Touch the rails or maybe don't touch the rails if you are like me. Are you being directed in this line, or can you choose where to go for yourself? What is the temperature like?

Imagine yourself at the front of the line now. One more group to go and then you will be next. The coaster cars pull in. You wait for the cars to clear and then you get the signal to get in. How do you feel? What is your heart doing? How is it beating? Feel your chest. Are your hands cold or clammy? How about your throat? Dry or wet? You get into the car. You pull the buckle over your lap and secure the safety bar. What are your thoughts? What are your thoughts about safety? Do you know what is going to happen? Have you done this before, or is this the first time? You are all buckled in. The "all clear" is given after some mumbled words about what to do and what not to do. What are you focused on? Are you looking ahead? Are you looking at the attendees? What are your thoughts? Are you looking at a friend, or is your head facing down? Where are your arms? Where are your legs? Where are your hands?

PARENTING WITH PIECES

The ride is starting. There is a jolt and hydraulic release as the rollercoaster inches forward. This is it. Jerk! Pull! Release! Push! Tug! Noises of other passengers range from yells, to shouts, to endless chatter. Are you silent? Are you participating in the vocal noise? The light changes as you leave the docking station and start your ascend. The cars are moving up. Gravity tells you that your orientation is changing.

I am going to give you some words and short phrases. Notice what you feel.

You are at the bottom.
Your back against the seat.
Middle.
Hands grip tightly.
Anticipation.
Wind.
Heart.
Seat.
Hope.
The ride stops.
Wait.
Feet.
Climb.
The ride continues.
Excitement.
Hair.
Fear.
Hands.
Breath.

High.

Head.

Calm.

Shift.

Joy.

Movement.

Rest.

Pause …

You have reached the top of the roller coaster and for a split second even the bravest of the brave think, "Oh My God! This Is Going To Happen!" You take a deep breath and …

Welcome back. Take a deep breath!

As you thought about that experience, or your own experience, how did you feel? Let me change the question and be more specific. How did your body react to the mental experience of riding on a roller coaster? What pictures did you see when a thought was placed in your head by the words on this page? Did you get tense? Did you have your own thoughts? Did your heart start beating a little faster? Did you believe you were there? Did your mind say that you were here, but your body said you were sitting on a rollercoaster? What came first, the thought, the emotion, or the feeling? Did they switch around? Could you tell the difference between one or the other? Did it flow together, or did you even notice?

Let's do this exercise a different way. I am going to suggest what your experience might have been. I am going to let you read the next paragraph and then I will explain what we are going to do after you are done. Go ahead and read the paragraph now.

When you decided to go on the rollercoaster …

Maybe you questioned your decision to get on the ride. You thought is this safe? Now, if you were questioning the decision, then your body probably tensed up, your heart rate went up, and you might have closed your eyes. Because of this physical reaction, you likely "felt" anxious, nervous, or regretful. If there was a threat of danger, perceived or actual, then your body likely reacted by your heart beat rising, you started to fidget, or started to babble or scream. Because of these reactions to the threat of danger, you may have "felt" scared, hostile, or panicked.

I am going to now go through this paragraph again and label the reactions. I am going to label thoughts, emotions, and feelings. I will use the terms mental, biochemical, and sensory. Bare with me and understand that many of these labels may have multiple answers. The point of this exercise is to see how our system works. Let's begin.

When you decided to go on the rollercoaster …

Maybe you questioned your decision to get on the ride (mental). **You thought is this safe** (mental)? **Now, if you were questioning the decision, then your body probably tensed up,** (biochemical) **your heart rate went up,** (biochemical) **and you**

might have closed your eyes (sensory protection). **Because of this physical reaction, you likely "felt" anxious,** (mental) **nervous,** (sensory and/or biochemical) **or regretful** (mental). **If there was a threat of danger,** (mental/biochemical) **perceived or actual,** (sensory) **then your body likely reacted by your heart beat rising,** (biochemical) **you started to fidget,** (sensory) **or started to babble or scream** (sensory/mental/biochemical). **Because of these reactions to the threat of danger, you may have "felt" scared,** (mental) **hostile,** (sensory) **or panicked** (biochemical/sensory).

This is an example of how your body starts reacting to stimulation. Normally, it does not even matter how it happens. This is why I do not want us to get hung up on the labels. We could spend a whole school semester learning and debating this topic. What we want to understand is that all of these parts flow back and forth to create an experience of life. When we want to direct or change the course of our experience we need to study and learn from ourselves as to what is actually going on and figure out how we should shift or direct these pieces.

Now, if you went on the roller coaster journey with me, then I want you to remember what it was like to go on that same ride again. Remember, you have done this before. Go back up to the exercise and read it again if that helps you. I will be here when you are ready.

Did the fact that you had already experienced the ride change anything? Were you able to have a different perspective now that you (and your system) had more understanding about what was taking place? Maybe you tried to put your hands up in the air this time. Maybe you saw more things around you. Was it different or the same? Think about this for a moment.

Thank you for going through all of this with me. I understand that you might be thinking, "What does this have to do with my child? Why do I need to do all this work?" I hope, by now, we have built a level of trust. I hope by the end of this book you can see how all of these seemingly separate topics flow together. You are doing a great job. Keep going. You are worth it.

Commitment First; Love Second

I hope you can see by now that feelings and emotions are ever changing. They are real. But our emotions and feelings (like pain and stress) are working for the sole purpose of automatically balancing our body's system. I want to also point out that I am not including thoughts. Thoughts are the one thing that you can control. They are the key that directs everything else. You will use thoughts; turning them into words; turning them into actions; in order to build a foundation you want. But here lies the question. Do you want to build a foundation on stress, pain, emotions, or feelings? You have a foundation of something. What I am trying to get you to do is select what your foundation is made of. This is why you need to know what makes you unique. All of this goes back to knowing yourself and your genius.

The EMOTIONS Piece

My husband and I worked diligently on the puzzle. We had been at this for several hours. The fireplace blazed and the cabin held us in a warm embrace. The carpet told the story of our long stay, and I shifted myself to another position allowing the crushed shag fabric and my knees a break. I looked over at my puzzle partner who was fixated in his process and could see the fatigue on his face. It had been a long day and I knew he must be tired.

"Feeling tired?" I asked.
"Nope! I'm fine," came the response.

A huge yawn immediately emerged from my denying mate. I offered for us to take a break and get some food, but my husband refused. I decided to take a break myself. I hunted around the unfamiliar kitchen. I opened several doors and drawers before finding the correct cooking utensils. I was glad to take a break from the puzzle. The winter rain continued to remind me of the good decision to remain indoors. A cold draft worked its way under the back door only to be swallowed up by the warmth of the cabin. I poked my head through the kitchen door to check on the progress of the puzzle. My husband was locked onto a particular section of the puzzle. He looked as if he was glued to his work.

"How's it going?"
"Fine."
"Did you find that piece for the sky?"
"Um, no thank you. I am still not hungry."

Obviously I, nor food, were the priorities. When the food was finished, I sat at the kitchen table eating alone. I could see my husband, and I smiled. The commitment he had for this puzzle was all-consuming. I finished my plate and took a hot drink to where my husband still sat in the living room. I knew that despite what he said, once he smelled any food or drink, he would want it. I broke his concentration.

"Hi."

"Hi." He reached for the hot drink. "Thank you."

"You're welcome. Are you sure you don't want to go to bed?"

"No, I started this and I want to finish it. I don't know why I let you talk me into this, but now I can't stop."

We laughed and I soon rejoined him on our mission. One thing I knew about my husband was that once he had an idea in his head he was not going to stop until he got what he wanted. He was fully committed to anything that he set his mind to do—including this puzzle.

As a professional in the field of family education and preservation, both socially and spiritually, I get the privilege of witnessing many different dynamics when it comes to family. I have witnessed thriving home environments. I have witnessed home environments that would have even the strongest people terrified and traumatized. I have (at the time of writing this book) worked in the child welfare system for over seventeen years and have been disciplined in spiritual education, teaching, and training for over twenty-five years. During this time, I have discovered that every relationship must have a foundation.

Every foundation must have commitment in order to survive and thrive.

Let's test this out. I am going to make a strong statement.

I am going to say, "Love is simply not enough to build a sustainable relationship."

You say, "What? That's all parenting is about—LOVE! What do you mean love isn't enough? Are you crazy?"

Let me explain.

Many would agree that love is an abstract term. This abstract term "Love" is often what we say our relational foundations are built on. But, since we cannot even agree what the term "Love" includes or does not include, we have a problem. What kind of love are you talking about? There are so many. Unconditional love? Parental love? Familial love? Romantic love? Sibling love? Love for country? Love for pizza? And within each of those categories we could have a hundred variations. Love, as we understand the term in its broadest scope, actually relies on unspoken and undefined principles that can be unrecognizable to all parties participating. I am not here to debunk love. I love love. I do want us to find a word, an idea, or a concept that is more concrete. I want something that has a clear definition. Relationships need concrete principles and consistency. Then, they need commitment. Terms and conditions apply and govern the commitment. Now you can see why I would say love—alone—is not enough.

My husband may not instantly have had love for our puzzle, but his commitment was unquestioned. And, as I would find out later, he really loved the experience. Did he love every part? I am sure that he did not. But his foundation was one of being a finisher. That is what he wanted to be known for; what he wanted to do; who he wanted to be, and he did what he needed to do to reach his goal and stay true to himself. His love for being a puzzle master came and went. Actually being a puzzle master was one of the ways he showed his deeper commitment or foundation of being a finisher.

Parenting can be the same. There are moments where you love being a parent and think that you could do this forever. There are other times where you pray that it will soon be over and dream of an empty nest. You did not come into this world saying, "I am a parent." You came into this world saying, "I am! I am me." This is why it is important to know your identity and from that identity will come your wants and desires. From those desires and wants come your larger foundation. That foundation holds your principles your ideas, your goals, and your dreams. Everything after that is just you practicing who you are through your life. You want to be committed to **You,** and then **You** can commit to your activities, jobs, loves, and life.

I would like your parenting experience to be focused on a commitment. I will let you set our own foundation as only you really know what you want to commit to. I hold no judgment and neither should you. Just know what you want from yourself and then commit. This is one of the reasons we spend so much time knowing ourselves. As we know more about ourselves we know more of what we want or what we want to commit to. I believe parenting should be more about the commitment you make, rather than the love you have to give. Love, like everything else, will build on your commitment.

You may say, "I already committed before I knew what I was committing to. I committed before I really knew anything about myself." Well, like my husband, you either decide that you like what you committed to and are willing to see it through or you change the commitment. But changing back and forth and not knowing what your commitment is will be damaging to yourself and to those around you. Again, I will go back to finding a foundation. What is the very core of what you want or who you are? Lock that in—commit to that idea, and build from there. When you seem lost, go back to your foundation. Go back to the commitment of that foundation. Go back again and again and again. You will, in time, reinforce your decision and know better how to get what you want. You will better know how to manipulate, change, shift, rearrange, or direct your life. I do not care what words you use as long as you understand the idea of what I am saying. I hope you can see that there are a lot of moving parts in a single situation, experience, or interaction. A change of direction in any one of these moving parts can cause a completely different outcome. Constant change creates instability. Instability does not promote growth.

Let's put this into context. In this example I am going to present two women. Each of these women have a foundation. These women have a foundation even if they are not conscience of what it is. Watch how they choose and navigate events in their life based on their foundation. But before we start, I want to point out that these women did not read my book. They do not know they have a cracked foundation. They do not know that much of the foundation they have committed to is hiding the best them. So, keep in mind how much easier life might be for these ladies if they chose a healthy foundation; a foundation that reflects what they want to create; a foundation from internal genius. Let's see how this plays out.

Denise wants safety and growth. Safety for Denise means bodily protection, and growth for Denise means mental and spiritual expansion.

Cindy wants security and happiness. Security for Cindy means economical and emotional stability, and happiness for Cindy means pleasurable temporal experiences.

They both want a child. They both would love to have a "little me" running around. They both dream of how the nursery would look and what activities they would do with their children. They want their children to thrive and succeed in life. They dream of watching their children grow up, get married, and have children of their own. How fun it will be at family get-togethers. So much love is in the future. They can't wait to get started.

Denise works to get pregnant and even though things are slow and unsuccessful at first she is not discouraged. Cindy gets pregnant quickly but loses the child early in the first trimester. This is a blow, but Cindy recovers and is willing to try again.

Both ladies struggle achieving their dream of being pregnant. Both start to feel like they might need to seek professional help. Denise finds out that pregnancy will be very difficult for her, and there is a possibility she will never have children. Cindy hears the same news. Here are their reactions.

Denise grieves. She then starts to look for alternatives. She researches in-vitro fertilization and adoption.

Cindy grieves. She also starts looking for alternatives. She researches in-vitro fertilization but will not consider adoption.

Why the different choices?

Denise's foundation is safety and growth so Denise is leery of the risks associated with in-vitro fertilization—however small. She has heard the horror stories and feels she is not willing to risk her body even if it is for a child she really wants. She needs to feel safe and yet she wants growth. Growth for Denise means starting a family. Since safety is her foundation and since she feels medical procedures are unsafe for her, adoption then seems like a good solution. Yes there are still unknowns, but they do not threaten her physical safety. Both criteria of safety and growth are met.

Cindy's foundation is security and happiness. Cindy looks at the risks associated with in-vitro fertilization as nothing because she feels secure with her doctor. She is not concerned at this point with safety as long as she feels secure. And she does. This is a slight difference but a difference nonetheless. Even if something were to go wrong with the medical procedure, she trusts her doctor to fix anything. She is even willing to suffer physically because she knows she has already gone through the loss of a child. She feels secure in her ability for her body to withstand anything she asks of it. And she is confident in her doctor. Adoption for Cindy has a lot more risk. She does not know the people who will come walking in and out of her life. At least with her doctor, she can get direct answers. Whenever she talks with adoption workers they give her vague unknowns. If she cannot feel comfortable with these people then she does not feel secure. Even if adoption could give her a child, she will not choose this option because of the insecurities it brings.

Denise is matched with a child and the adoption is finalized.
Cindy gives birth to a healthy child.
Both women have what they want—a baby.

These two ladies start the process of raising their wonderful children. Denise is a bit protective. She wants her child to stay close by her side. Often playdates and social activities are limited. This, of course, makes sense because Denise values safety. The adoption process was not quite as safe as she would hope for. Some of the people she encountered were hostile, and there were quite a few run-ins with the birth mother. This taught Denise that not all people have her priority of safety. She is on high alert. However, there is also something else she wants. She wants her child to grow. Denise feels a bit torn because on the one hand she wants her child to be safe, but on the other hand she wants her child to have as many growth developing opportunities as she can. So Denise finds the solution in many activities that involve both her and her child. As long as Denise can physically see her child and know that she is safe then she is willing and wants her child to do just about anything. Denise really struggles with parents who just let their children wander off. Denise would never let that happen. She is starting to become overprotective and fearful when it comes to her child. She may start displaying aggressive behaviors to other adults who interact with her child. There are many locks on the doors at home, and anything deemed unsafe is removed from the child's environment.

Cindy is thrilled with her new child. The procedure went well which reinforced Cindy's security in her doctor and that she made the right choice. Cindy feels like life has given her both security and happiness. She has what she wants. She starts filling her life with happy things and fun activities. She plans parties, playdates, trips to the beach, and anything that she can imagine. She starts spending a lot of money on toys and clothes for her child. When faced with the decision to do something educational or fun, Cindy will always choose the fun activity. In fact, her school of choice is based on how fun the teachers are and how much happiness is brought into the classroom. Cindy cries and cries the first day of school. She is going to miss her child so much. She feels insecure not having her child by her side. She feels like she does not know what to do with herself. She has started to identify more as a mother than as an individual person. She finds security in the title of mother and the expectations of being a mother. She loves her role and talks about her child all the time. Her friends start to distance themselves due to Cindy's constant bombardment of pictures and videos. Her friends try to get her to have a girl's night out, but going out by herself without her child makes Cindy feel insecure. Cindy stays home more and more.

Denise is wearing herself out. She is constantly on the run doing activities with her child. She feels like she needs a break. Denise has had many offers from other parents to help out but Denise, up to this point, has refused. Denise just does not feel it is safe. Denise gets a flyer from her child's teacher telling of an upcoming field trip. There is a conflict on Denise's schedule, and she almost refuses to sign the parent release form. Something stops her. Denise knows that this field trip will be a growing experience for her child. She knows that the school and the teachers will keep everyone safe. She has learned to trust the other parents in her child's class. Denise takes a big step and lets her child go by herself on the field trip. Denise is not happy about having to make a decision between her personal version of safety and the growth of her child. But Denise is tired of always having to keep her child safe. She has seen how sometimes her child really wants to learn and experience new things, but Denise has stopped her child because of Denise's own fear about safety. Denise knows it is time to start letting her child experience their own version of growth.

Cindy knows that she has to get her budget under control. She has known this for a long time. She just has such a hard time resisting those cute outfits. Shopping makes Cindy so happy. However, the low bank account is making Cindy feel insecure. Cindy starts selling off many of the toys, and her child seems to be just fine either way. Cindy realizes that her child can be happy with less. With this sudden interest in a financial future, Cindy starts looking at her daughter's "proper" education as a way to secure a long and happy life. She enrolls her child in private school with very strict standards. Having fun is not so much a priority now because Cindy is more concerned with security at this moment. Cindy wants her child to have a solid education so she can have a happy future.

Both children are relatively happy and well balanced. The time comes for college and the children are ready to pick which school they want to attend and what they will be studying.

Denise wants her child to go to a school nearby but really does not care what her child studies. As long as they are growing, they are free to choose what they want. There has been some talk even of skipping school and taking a year off to go travel the world and have fun. Denise thinks she is good with this as long as she knows where her child will be and can do some research on the places in question. However, she really wants her child to stay nearby. Denise even has thought about moving wherever her child ends up going to school. She would be willing to leave her job which she has held for fifteen years. Many choices need to be made and they need to be made soon.

Cindy has it all planned out—where her child is going to go and what her child is going to study. Everything is perfect. Cindy is very happy for her child because her child can easily get into one of the top schools in the country. Every grooming opportunity that Cindy never had has been given to her child.

Cindy is happy and secure. Her child has turned out quite well. There will be some sadness when her child leaves for university, but it will be worth it. Cindy likes telling people that her child will be attending this prestigious school. She almost feels like she is the one attending and is very proud of her child.

The children go off to school without much trouble.

Denise's child chose a school out of state. Denise decided not to move but visits often. She is known by all of her child's friends as THE mom. Denise likes the title and likes mothering the friends of her child. She sends care packages regularly. When visiting (much to her child's displeasure) she sneaks into her child's dorm room to do laundry and clean. The months that Denise is away from her child are difficult for her, but she is happy that her child is learning so much. She is proud of who her child is becoming and is willing to allow this process.

Cindy seems to be blossoming now that her child is off to school. Cindy rarely visits because she does not see the need. She seems to do well with one phone call a month. Her priority is on the child's report cards. So far, so good. Cindy's social life is full and she has many new friends. She got a promotion at work and has gone on several shopping sprees. She feels she has done a good job in her life and is very happy. There is even talk of her child dating. This promise thrills Cindy.

The children come home for a holiday and introduce the persons they have been dating. Denise and Cindy are shocked. They had no idea that their children had been dating outside of their ethnicity. Denise and Cindy are not happy. Both parents have the same reaction but for different reasons. The question is;

"Why are you doing this TO ME?"

When Denise says this, she means why are you threatening my safety. I didn't have time to see if this is safe. You know I don't like surprises. We don't know anything about this person or culture. This is not what I expected for me. Where will you live? What will happen to me? Will I be accepted into this new world that you (the child) are creating for yourself?

When Cindy says this question, she means this doesn't make me happy. Being unhappy makes me feel insecure. This is not what I had planned for me. I wouldn't choose this for myself so why would you choose it for you? I worked so hard to give you (the child) what would make me happy. Now you are telling me that **you** are unhappy? This makes me even more insecure because it means I might not have made the right choices. I do not like this feeling. There are so many choices that would make me happy but this is not one of them.

"Why would you do this to me?" Same question from two different foundations.

Then Denise's child starts to reassure Denise that everything is alright. After some time Denise gets to know this person her child is dating. Denise feels safer with this idea and she really sees how her child is growing into a wonderful unique individual. Denise sees safety and growth for her child. She agrees to this relationship and comes around to support it in the end.

Cindy listens to her child persuade her that this person is perfect for them. Cindy sees how happy her child is but still is reluctant. She now has a choice between her happiness and her child's happiness. Until this point, she had viewed them as one and the same. Even though her child had fought her on several decisions during childhood, Cindy usually got her way and thought everything was great. Now she was hearing that her child wanted something different. How could this be? But Cindy also heard something else. She heard how this person her child was dating had a very promising career. She heard how stable s/he was as a person and how her/his family was reputable. Cindy started to come around. She started to notice how happy her child really was. This was not Cindy's first choice, but it was a choice she could get used to. Cindy could see that her child was secure and happy. Cindy gave her blessing for this relationship.

While these two stories could have had so many different twists and turns, I hope you can see the point. The foundation that each parent chose directed their decisions. Life was not just happening to them. Underneath the surface, choices were being made based on their foundation. The moments that were "difficult" for each parent were times that events in life seemed to threaten the parent's foundation. The "threat" really had nothing to do with the child's well-being. The threat was against the parent's foundation.

The EMOTIONS Piece

There is no right or wrong foundation. You may (as I do) have an opinion about each parent, but that is really irrelevant for the sake of this lesson. We actually are only viewing this story from our own foundations. The point is to look at what is the motivating or driving force behind each decision.

What I am asking for you is to understand your foundation. More than that, I want you to choose your foundation for yourself. Then commit to your foundation. This is where the self-work comes in. This is why I will continue to ask you who are you and what do you want? I want to remove fear from this process. You will get this in time.

Chapter 6: The EMOTIONS Piece
Placing The Pieces

Based upon this chapter:

1: What is your foundation?

_____

_____

2: How do you express your foundation?

_____

_____

3: What rules or practices are inconsistent with your foundation?

_____

_____

4: What are ways you can refocus your foundation with your practice?

_____

_____

Honor Yourself. I acknowledge that I am doing well in some areas, and I agree to continually educate and improve myself where needed.

_____   _____
Name   Date

Chapter 7

The CONFRONTATION Piece

ဆ

"Remember, confrontation is about
reconciliation and awareness,
not judgement or anger."
- Dale Partridge[26] -

Making Your Choice

The three boys were lined up ready to receive their yogurt. Ever since I worked as the Manager of Store Openings for a California based yogurt company, yogurt has replaced our ice-cream. How exciting! Each boy could choose any flavor they wanted, and as much as they wanted, as long as it could be contained within their yogurt bowl. Flavor after flavor spread out before them inviting them to choose, choose, choose. Large chilled stainless steel containers poked out the openings in the wall. Their nozzles just waiting to be pulled. One of the nice things about these stores was that you could sample the flavors before you committed to a bowl full of one particular flavor. Now, my boys are usually very direct. Separately, they have a very clear vision of who they are and what they want. Lack of expression has never been an issue in our house—believe me. However, this particular day a strange phenomena took place. A banter started between my boys. The moment one child seemed to decide on which flavor was best for him, the other two would discredit the decision.

"Are you sure you want that one?"
"Don't forget about this one!"
"I think this one is better."
"Why don't you try this one again before you choose."
"You don't really like that do you?"
"You like this one."
"This is your favorite."

What was interesting was that there seemed to be no logic to any of the statements other than to dissuade the confident brother of his choice. For in fact, not two seconds later, the same boy questioning his brother would make a statement like:

"Oh wow, that **is** really good. Maybe I should try that."

Of course, as soon as this was said, the other two would jump in and challenge the wisdom of that thought. There was constant contradiction even in their own statements. They backtracked and wandered around the subject of yogurt with no clear solution to any of their questions. It seemed to me, as if the point of the heckling was to get the other person to second guess their decision not actually help the person in making their decision. I finally gave them all a time limit. There were now quite a few people waiting behind us.

"I am going to count to ten. Pick what you want or I will pick for you."

Within seconds each had chosen their favorite flavor, and every boy had chosen the flavor he had originally wanted.

Do you ever feel confronted? Have you ever had the experience of being questioned about your parenting? We as parents are not usually sensitive to other parents. We of course believe our choices are the best. We usually are free to express this belief to other parents. And we don't just have one opinion. Oh no. We have an opinion on everything and everyone. We have an opinion on what clothes are best to wear and what games are best to play. Even those parents who hold that they do not have any opinions, turn around and make opinions about those who do have opinions. I remember my husband coming home one day from picking our oldest up from school. He had endured a particularly rigorous parental judging session while waiting for our son. When he got home he said, "I just wish all the parents would leave each other alone. I don't think parents ever grow up. It's just like being on the playground again."

The truth is that sometimes you are under the microscope of society. How can we work this to our advantage? Well, this can serve to improve how you think and thrive as a parent. You can manage your own responses and behaviors to society. Yes, you must train others how to treat you, but first, you must train yourself how to respond when others confront you. This process is about learning how to **respond** to people versus **reacting** to people.

What happens when you are confronted? Do you feel judgmental and angry or do you look for ways to resolve the situation and improve the next set of interactions? Learning from the chapter on stress, we can see how if we are reacting this defensively then most likely we feel threatened. Our body says that there is danger up ahead. Reviewing what we learned from our chapter on emotions, we can see how we could easily start reacting out of impulse if we do not quickly take control and direct ourselves to a positive outcome.

The CONFRONTATION Piece

Usually we react to something or someone when it offends us. Sometimes, reacting is our way of asserting ourselves and gaining back control. Reacting to every confrontation can cause us to be defensive. Parents need physical, spiritual, and certainly emotional rest. Being on the defensive does not allow you to find rest because you are constantly waiting for the next attack.

What is confrontation? Really it just means that we are meeting something face to face. Some thing, idea, or person stands in our path and says. "here I am". Many times we do not like this and so we react negatively. But we should take a look to see if we are bothered because of **what** is standing in our path or the fact that something **is** standing in our path. There really are two options when you are confronted:

1: Rejection

When we reject something, we are saying this is not safe for me. The way we express this rejection is where we spend most of our time. Just like our systems, we have many ways to respond to rejection. We can defend against it. We can attack it. We can avoid it. We can become angry, hostile, passive, or silent. We can seek revenge, justice, support, explanation, fortification and apology. There are so many ways that we deal with something we want to reject. We are very creative beings. However, all of this has to do with rejecting the idea, situation or person.

2: Acceptance

When we accept the idea, situation or person we are saying, "Yes, you are safe for me. I see no threat to what is standing in my path." We can express this with love, joy, warmth, and sympathy. We can adopt, adapt, welcome, and join. Again, the ways we can show acceptance are many and various.

So what should we choose? Ah, the fun part. Ready for some questions? Find out what is going on.

1. Are you really under attack?
2. Is this a real threat or a perceived threat?
3. If this is a real threat, what exactly is being threatened?
4. What are the best and most effective ways to protect what is being threatened?
5. What do you want to do about this attack?
6. Will your solution to this attack end the threat or will it induce more attack?
7. Can you sustain your decision or do you have the power and resources to back your decision?
8. Will this attack repeat?

I would like to go back to our parents Denise and Cindy. Remember that Denise wanted safety and growth and Cindy wanted security and happiness. Let's for a moment pretend that both parents lived on the same street. Their children are the same age and have just turned six. Denise invites Cindy over to the house for an afternoon playdate. While they are sitting around watching their children, a conversation begins about the new park going in at the end of the street. Denise, of course, gets up several times during the conversation to check on the children playing nicely in the other room. The conversation may go something like this;

The CONFRONTATION Piece

Denise: Did you hear about the park going in near Dearborn Street?

Cindy: I did. I actually was on the park committee that sponsored it.

Denise: I didn't know that.

Cindy: They were going to put it over on Lakewood, but they didn't know if the entrances were going to meet city codes.

Denise: Oh, Lakewood is closer to my house. That would have been nice.

Cindy: Yes, it would have been nice, but there have to be two entrances into the park, and that would have required bulldozing one of the houses.

Denise: I don't see why they can't just make an exception. It would be a whole lot safer to have the park on this side of the neighborhood than having to cross that big intersection over on Dearborn.

Cindy: Well, at the Dearborn location they can build a bigger playground and are even talking about putting in a kiddy fountain.

Denise: A kiddy fountain? I have heard those things can be dangerous. Just the other day there was a report on the news about bacteria building up in the pipes and getting the children sick.

Cindy: Yes, but that will happen to anything if it isn't properly cared for. I'm not going to let a little bacteria get in the way of my child's fun.

Denise: Why not put that money to the new wing of the library? Heaven knows they could use the funds.

Cindy: Oh that's no fun. I'd rather play in a fountain any day than read an old book.

Denise: You don't mean that. I thought you would love books. You seem so smart.

Cindy: Just because I'm smart doesn't mean that I can't have fun.

Denise: Well, nothing is fun when you're in the hospital with an infection.

Cindy: Well, I supposed we could all just sit around reading books then.

Denise: Books never hurt anyone.

Cindy: Unless you count getting a paper cut or dropping a book on your foot.

Denise: My child is not that careless.

Cindy: I'm just saying accidents happen.

Denise: Like at kiddy fountains.

Cindy: Why do you always have to be such a party pooper?

Denise: I'm not a party pooper. I just like to be safe.

Cindy: And I like to have fun. I don't see the harm.

Denise: I like fun.

Cindy: Then come with me to the new farmer's market. I hear they have a cute guy working the coffee stand.

Denise: I don't want to flirt with the coffee guy.

Cindy: Afraid of a little danger?

Denise: Not afraid—just smart. I would like to be around for a while, and tramping around town with who knows who can't end well.

Cindy: Life doesn't have to be so serious all the time.

Denise: And life isn't one big game.

Cindy: It could be, if you let it.

Now, this conversation goes on, but I will step in for a moment. Do you see what is happening? Even between friends there is an undertow of combative sparing. Really this conversation is pitting Denise's safety against Cindy's fun. Both ladies are not going to change their foundation. Denise will always choose safety and Cindy will always choose fun. If these ladies are not careful they could find themselves in a serious war over which foundation will win. Denise and Cindy might start seeing each other as a threat to the each other. Unchecked, some serious attacks might be made simply because each person is trying to protect themselves. They have both chosen to take a rejection stance rather than an acceptance stance. Truth be told, we can see value in both stances. However, if Denise and Cindy know very much about each other and if they know something about themselves, the conversation could go something like this;

Denise: Did you hear about the park going in near Dearborn Street?

Cindy: I did. I actually was on the park committee that sponsored it.

Denise: I didn't know that.

Cindy: They were going to put it over on Lakewood but they didn't know if the entrances were going to meet city code.

Denise: Oh, Lakewood is closer to my house. That would have been nice.

Cindy: Yes, it would have been nice but there have to be two entrances into the park, and that would have required bulldozing one of the houses.

Denise: I don't see why they can't just make an exception. It would be a whole lot safer to have the park on this side of the neighborhood than having to cross that big intersection over on Dearborn.

Cindy: Well at the Dearborn location they can build a bigger playground and are even talking about putting in a kiddy fountain.

Denise: A kiddy fountain? I have heard those things can be dangerous. Just the other day there was a report on the news about bacteria building up in the pipes and getting the children sick.

Cindy: I think that is why they are holding off on the installation. They want to make sure its safe. Even though I would love to see a kiddy fountain go in, I understand the concern.

Denise: Why not put that money to the new wing of the library? Heaven knows they could use the funds.

Cindy: Well the library has its own funds, and the park committee has been saving this money for several years.

Denise: You know, I think that's really good. The library could really learn from their example.

Cindy: It wasn't easy, but the parks and recreations department really has done a good job trying to choose a safe spot for the park as well as making sure they have enough funds to keep up the park for several years.

Denise: That's why I like this new park administrator, it seems he knows what he is doing.

Cindy: Well, he makes me feel secure.

Denise: Agreed.

Cindy: Hey you should come with me to the new farmer's market. I hear they have a cute guy working the coffee stand.

Denise: I don't want to flirt with the coffee guy.

Cindy: Ok, well you shop for healthy food, and I'll flirt with the coffee guy.

Denise: Must I always keep you safe.

Cindy: Yes. And must I always make you have fun?

Denise: Probably.

Cindy: So, I'll see you next Saturday?

Denise: I'll buy you a cup of coffee.

This is a very different conversation. The difference is that they found a line of conversation that joined what they most had in common—that of safety and security. Notice, they also had a level of acceptance of each other which allowed them to be flexible with the differences between them. The second conversation seemed less confrontational and formed around what they **could** agree on, even if it was just a few things. These two woman will have a much healthier relationship choosing an acceptance stance rather than a rejection stance. And as this relationship grows and trust is built between these two ladies, they can learn to reject an idea of the other person without having to reject the person giving the idea. They can learn that the idea and the person are not the same. They are training their systems how to properly place the confrontation piece.

Chapter 7: The CONFRONTATION Piece
Placing The Pieces

Based upon this chapter:

1:   What is one thing you will remember from this chapter?

_____

_____

2:   What times do you most feel attacked?

_____

_____

3:   What is a threat that might be a perceived threat rather than a real threat?

_____

_____

4:   What is being threatened?

_____

_____

5:   What ways do you want to choose to protect yourself?

_____

_____

6:   Will your plan keep this attack from happening again?

_____

_____

7:   How will you help yourself in the moment of the attack to keep to your plan?

_____

_____

8:   What is your foundation?

_____

_____

9:   What are ways to protect your foundation without attacking?

_____

_____

10:   What is working in the conversations you have with people?

_____

_____

11: What do you want to improve on?

_____

_____

Honor Yourself. I acknowledge that I am doing well in some areas, and I agree to continually educate and improve myself where needed.

_____   _____

Name   Date

Chapter 8

The READY Piece

෪

"We keep moving forward, opening new doors,
and doing new things, because we're curious and
curiosity keeps leading us down new paths."
- Walt Disney[27] -

Letting Curiosity Lead

The box sat there on the floor. It was late. We had been at this for hours. Had it not been for my willful husband, I would have long since been in bed. But what we started we would finish. There was the box promising me of my reward if I kept a steady course. I knew I could do this. I looked over at the box occasionally to verify that I was going in the right path. Sometimes I challenged its correctness. Even though I knew what the picture of this puzzle was supposed to look like, watching it take form was somehow different than what I had expected. I saw the picture on the box, but what was this thing fitting together on the floor in front of me? How was this all going to fit together? Sections were very clear. I had all the parts and I knew what it was going to be. Yet some places of the puzzle seemed confusing. Colors seemed to float and blend into each other for no apparent reason. Some shapes of the pieces actually fit together but the pattern on the pieces itself was far from a match. I looked over at my husband who by now was finishing up his section of the puzzle. How would his part and my part fit together? There was a growing anticipation of what was going to come. You could say we had a curiosity that drove us. What fit next? Where were we going? Would we like what we had when we finished?

I want you to look at parenting like a puzzle. Who knows where you are going to go or what you are going to do? All you can do is fit the next puzzle piece in a place that seems best. You might find a "fit" and then realize that the picture does not match—so you try again. Some of the colors might seem to match but the shape does not allow for a clean union. You try again. You keep trying. You take a break, and then you try some more. You get help when you need it; a fresh perspective; a helping hand. Little by little, a picture forms that is breathtaking and profoundly you. Even if there is a picture on the "box"—a picture of who you might be—there is nothing like the real thing. There is nothing like the real you laid out before your own eyes. It is thrilling and inspiring.

I could have waited for a better time—sure. Yes, we would be better prepared tomorrow—maybe. I could have asked if this night was really the right time to be starting a puzzle? Had we not been through enough of our own personal trauma from the day? We both had not done a puzzle for years. We did not seem like puzzle masters. Who were we to start on this adventure? How did we know that all the pieces were even there? What if we were not good at putting together the puzzle? What if, what if, what if …

There is an old proverb that says, "When the will is ready, the feet are light."

Waiting around till you are ready to be a good parent is like waiting to eat until you are full. You will never be full if you do not start eating. How you eat, when you eat, and what you eat are totally different questions. I want to remind you again that you can do this. You have everything that it takes. You will get better and better as you grow into yourself more and more. I want you to strive for growth. You have as much as you need for this day. Tomorrow you will have enough for tomorrow. Keep focused on the moment. Keep focused on you in the moment and your curiosity will guide you in the right direction. You learn to move forward, not because you are ready—but because you have a right to grow into yourself. The truth is we are never ready and are always ready at the same time.

Proud of the Process

The birds were loud. They announced the new day with such vigor that one would think some dignitary was nearby. The rain had ceased and the trees stretched their branches up to the blue heavens. Morning. The night had blended into the day and we woke up before the kids. Had it been a dream? Did we do what we thought we had done? All was true. All was right. There it was before us. No dream, just the pure puzzle finished and waiting an approving gaze.

We wanted to show the boys what we had done. We were proud of our puzzle that was beautifully laid out on the living room floor. There were instructions to the boys on how to enter the living room. My husband and I valued this puzzle. This was not just any puzzle. It was **OUR** puzzle. **We** did this. We **loved** it. No one could take that feeling away from us. Our boys were not to touch this puzzle. "Just look at it," came the instruction.

All of the pain and struggle of the previous day was washed away with the rain. Our puzzle was worth every confused and conflicting moment. A beautiful landscape was before us. Within the borders of this puzzle stood several country buildings set against the bright vivid contrast of fall trees and deep blue sky. A work to behold. The boys had given the obligatory, "That's cool," and then rushed off to breakfast.

Now what? Now what do we do? We both knew the answer. We wanted to build another puzzle. We did not want to dismantle this puzzle but we sure wanted to continue our adventure. We were hooked. You would think that we would be finished. That all that work would have deterred us from ever wanting to do a puzzle again. But the opposite was true. We wanted more. The best part about putting the puzzle together was in fact putting the puzzle together. We were proud of the process. What about you?

All good things do not always have to come to an end, and I certainly hope this is the case for the progress you have made on this journey. What a ride this has been with you. I want to thank you for partnering with me on this journey.

Parenting is, in fact, one of the greatest rides you will ever take. Parenting is a ride that will have its ups and downs; its twists and turns; its joys and sorrows. And in the moments of putting the puzzle together, it will be tempting to finish the puzzle fast.

Look, parenting is a hard job and tough business. Parenting has been said, by many, to be the hardest job in the world. Any person that has the hardest job in the world probably needs a break. It is typical to look for the light at the end of the tunnel and imagine when "one day," it will all be over. As weird as it may sound, one day you might look back and wish you had these moments again. You may wish that you were starting your puzzle anew. Yes, parenting takes a lot from you but it also **makes** a lot **of** you. Parenting takes all the pieces of your life and pushes you to make beautiful moments you will remember. The bigger picture of parenting is not about creating a work of perfection. Parenting is about the pieces you find along the journey, the wonderfully fulfilling work, and the picture you create at the end. But is it the end?

Chapter 8: The READY Piece
Placing The Pieces

Based upon this chapter:

1: What is one thing you will remember that impacted you?

_____

_____

2: What is working?

_____

_____

3: What is one thing you are doing well?

_____

_____

4: What is not working?

_____

_____

5: What is one thing you can improve?

_____

_____

6:   What is "missing?"

_____

_____

7:   What do you think you need to improve it?

_____

_____

Honor Yourself. I acknowledge that I am doing well in some areas, and I agree to continually educate and improve myself where needed.

_____   _____

Name   Date

Conclusion

ഔ

"It is good to have an end to journey toward;
but it is the journey that matters, in the end."
- Ernest Hemingway[28] -

The Journey Matters

I want you, as we end this part of our journey, to know that we have just begun. You are never finished, and you never want to be. You will always be looking at new pieces. You will always be asking where do I want to be? You will have fun discovering and rearranging the pieces until they better fit into place.

I trust that this book has helped you start or continue on the path of knowing yourself. I hope you have learned how to look, listen, and try when it comes to knowing who you are. I know you are going to be an expert at seeing the piece for what it actually is and not just what others say it is. I know you are capable of identifying your needs and then constructing a path to get from where you are to where you want to be.

You have what it takes to get the perspective you want. Ask yourself daily, "What is at the heart of what I want? What is my intent?" Let go of those policies, rules, and regulations that do not work for you. Focus on your core foundation, and learn to broaden and deepen that foundation. Understand that there are no missing pieces in your life, and release yourself from the pressure that obligation demands. Find the edges or boundaries of your specific life's puzzle, and use comparisons wisely. Remember all examples are for your good—to build you up. The world holds many ideas of how you can succeed as a parent. Pick the ideas that inspire you, and fuel your curiosity to learn and grow. You are unique and a genius in your own right.

You know your abilities, and you will use the information that you learn to make clear sustainable decisions for your future. Your identity is not just what other people label you as, but you are internally focused and always bringing out more of yourself. You are creating life on your terms! You acknowledge the strengths that others see in you and find opportunities to own those strengths and use them for your growth. When you get stuck trying to fit a piece into a spot that does not work, you are not afraid to rearrange that piece and try it in another place. You view all questions as a path to finding out more of who you are and what you want. You are good at recognizing stress, and you know how to listen to pain. You work with your body helping it understand where you are going and what you intend. You are patient with yourself and allow time to adjust and rest. You are better at discerning your feelings, thoughts, and emotions. **You know you are the puzzle master and the creator of your own life.** You are proud of what you do and where you have come from. I am proud of you. I know you can do this.

Yes, you are a parent. And, you are a great parent at that. You are getting better at being a parent every day. Keep up the good work. Thank you for allowing me into your life. Thank you for allowing me to walk with you in this process. I am sure we will converse and connect again. We are all here for a reason and for a purpose. We all have something to give. We deserve to be able to become ourselves. We need each other to be the best of ourselves. I need you to be the best you and you need me to be the best me. Only then can we support and sustain the larger puzzle of life. I look forward to seeing what you create.

Here's to your journey of Parenting With Pieces!

Acknowledgements

ဆာ

It Takes A Village

They say, "it takes a village to raise a child," and in many ways writing a book also takes a village. Even this is an understatement. I am privileged to have a village that has supported me throughout the entire process of this book.

I want to thank and acknowledge everyone that supported me, the creation of this book, and its related products. I want to give a special thanks and appreciate to my support team who are all listed below. I have received encouragement from many sources along the way however my team has played a vital role in the making and manifestation of this book. For this I am eternally grateful.

To Jeremy James Witcher:
Words cannot express the deep love I have for you. I appreciate your hard work and diligence throughout this entire process. You have been relentless and have helped motivate me through every step of this book. Thank you for the long brainstorming sessions, late night conversations, and countless times you went back to the drawing board with me. I could not have done this without you. Thank you for taking this journey of life and parenthood with me. I watch you continually grow as a person and parent every day and for that I am proud to be your husband. I look forward to our life together as we continue

to build our family. Here's to an eternity of creating the life we want full of love, happiness, peace, and joy—together. I love you always and in all ways.

To Bennie Mayberry:

Thank you for the dedication and intensity that you brought to this project. My life has truly been enriched since we have become friends. Thank you for continually believing in me and continually showing your support. Your expertise and insights have been invaluable to me, and I am sincerely grateful for your gift and generosity. Having a friend like you makes the journey more exciting, definitely interesting, and a whole lot easier. I look forward witnessing and supporting the creations you bring forth. I love you very much.

To Shell Taylor:

It is a privilege to call you a friend. From the very start you have been nothing but encouraging to me and for that I thank you. Thank you for your expertise as an author and your guidance. I also appreciate your willingness to keep me accountable and focused on writing. The clarity that you brought to editing was priceless and I truly thank you. I wish continued success for you and your family.

To Jonathan Hanneman:

Thank you for offering your time in reviewing and editing this book. I am grateful for the honesty, commitment, and quality you provided our team. I also want to thank your family for allowing me to borrow you for a few hours!

To Amy Mucken:

What can I say my dear? You are definitely a friend that is in it for the long haul. You have always freely given of yourself and your time, and I appreciate it from the bottom of my heart. I know the sacrifice that you made by giving time to this project, and for that, you have my eternal gratitude and thanks. Your support is unquestionable, your dedication is admirable, and you have left me speechless. I pray that your life is continually filled with unlimited joy, love, and success.

To Dr. Carlton D. Pearson:

You have always been a mentor and spiritual icon to me. I remember watching you on television as a child and hoping some day I would get a chance to meet you. Dreams do come true. Even with your busy schedule you have always made time for me. I am always appreciative. You have been an example and encouragement for me in some of my most trying spiritual transitions. Thank you for the personal impact you have made to my life and my family. Your contributions to our world will always be remembered. Thank you for being a colleague, mentor, and friend. My love always remains with you and your family.

To Tammy Felicia Rae Witcher:

Thank you for being the best sister ever! You have been supportive in all of my endeavors—I thank you. I appreciate your encouragement in this book. Continue to be your loving and sweet self. I also commend you for the dedication as a mother. I love you.

To Vivian Joyce Witcher (aka Mom):

Thank you mom for all you are and for everything you have done for me. You have supported me throughout my life, and I truly appreciate it. I know it was not easy being a single mom and raising me, but you did an excellent job. You should be extremely proud of yourself. I imagine that many times you felt discouraged but let this book stand as proof that your hard work paid off. I attribute all of my past, present, and future success to the foundation and faith you instilled into me as your child. I'm sure that Grandma and Grandpa are very proud of you as well. Thank you for teaching me how to be a committed and confident man. I love you more than words can express.

To Stella Mae Witcher (aka Grandma):

And finally … Thank you grandma for the spiritual deposit that you placed in my life from an early age. I continually pull from the well of your love and knowledge. You are my eternal supporter and my cheerleader behind the scenes. In all of my efforts I hear you saying "Good job 'pretty'!" Thank you for your life you shared with all of us! I miss you but acknowledge your ever-present spirit. I trust I am making you proud.

A Special Thanks To
The *Parenting with Pieces* Team

Contributing Editor
Jeremy Witcher

Marketing Consultant
Bennie Mayberry

Editors
Shell Taylor
Jonathan Hanneman
Amy Mucken

Foreword
Dr. Carlton D. Pearson

My Sister & Supporter
Tammy Felicia Rae Witcher

My Original Supporter
Vivian Witcher (*aka* Mom)

My Eternal Supporter
Stella Mae Witcher (*aka* Grandma)

The Parenting Pieces

The PERSPECTIVE Piece
The GENIUS Piece
The IDENTITY Piece
The STRESS Piece
The EMOTIONS Piece
The CONFRONTATION Piece
The EXPECTATIONS Piece
The READY Piece

www.ParentingWithPieces.com

*Subscribe to our mailing list and
Join our online community*

Notes

Preface

1. parent. Dictionary.com. Online Etymology Dictionary. Douglas Harper, Historian. http://dictionary.reference.com/browse/parent (accessed: July 23, 2015).

Introduction

2. Aristotle. "Aristotle Quotes". GoodReads.com. http://www.goodreads.com/author/show/2192.Aristotle (accessed: July 29, 2015).

Chapter 1
The PERSPECTIVE Piece

3. Furtick, Steven. It's In Your Hands, It's In Your Hands. Podcast video. Elevation Church. 21:50. https://itunes.apple.com/us/podcast/its-in-your-hands-its-in-your/id444092800?i=345374610&mt=2. (accessed: August 30, 2015).
4 . Furtick, Steven. It's In Your Hands, It's In Your Hands. Podcast video. Elevation Church. 21:50. https://itunes.apple.com/us/podcast/its-in-your-hands-its-in-your/id444092800?i=345374610&mt=2. (accessed: August 30, 2015).

Chapter 2
The EXPECTATIONS Piece

5. Stephen R. Covey. "Stephen R. Covey Quotes". GoodReads.com. http://www.goodreads.com/author/show/1538.Stephen_R_Covey (accessed: July 22, 2015).

Chapter 3
The GENIUS Piece

6. Murdock, Mike. "The Law of Difference." In 7 Laws You Must Honor To Have Uncommon Success. (Denton, TX: Wisdom Center, 2010).

7 . Albert Einstein. "Albert Einstein Quotes". BrainyQuotes.com. http://www.brainyquote.com/quotes/authors/a/albert_einstein.html (accessed: July 21, 2015).

8 . Michelangelo. "Michelangelo Quotes". BrainyQuotes.com. http://www.brainyquote.com/quotes/authors/m/michelangelo.html (accessed: July 21, 2015).

Chapter 4
The IDENTITY Piece

9. RuPaul. "RuPaul Quotes". GoodReads.com. http://www.goodreads.com/author/show/180188.RuPaul (accessed: August 25, 2015).

10 . noun. Dictionary.com. Dictionary.com Unabridged. Random House, Inc. http://dictionary.reference.com/browse/noun (accessed: July 21, 2015).

11 . Deepak Chopra. "Deepak Chopra Quotes". GoodReads.com. https://www.goodreads.com/author/show/138207.Deepak_Chopra (accessed: September 30, 2015).

12 . Benjamin Disraeli. BrainyQuote.com, Xplore Inc, 2015. http://www.brainyquote.com/quotes/quotes/b/benjamindi154148.html, accessed October 1, 2015.

13 . John C. Maxwell. "John C. Maxwell Quotes". GoodReads.com. https://www.goodreads.com/author/show/68.John_C_Maxwell (accessed: September 30, 2015).

14 . Max Planck. "Max Planck Quotes". GoodReads.com. http://www.goodreads.com/author/quotes/107032.Max_Planck (accessed: September 30, 2015).

15 . Wayne W. Dyer. "Wayne W. Dyer Quotes". GoodReads.com. http://www.goodreads.com/author/quotes/2960.Wayne_W_Dyer (accessed: September 30, 2015).

Chapter 5
The STRESS Piece

16. Fred Rogers (Author of The World According to Mister Rogers). "Fred Rogers Quotes". GoodReads.com. http://www.goodreads.com/author/quotes/32106.Fred_Rogers (accessed: July 20, 2015).

17 . Wikipedia contributors, "Mister Rogers' Neighborhood," Wikipedia, The Free Encyclopedia, https://en.wikipedia.org/w/index.

php?title=Mister_Rogers%27_Neighborhood&oldid=668717169 (accessed July 20, 2015).

18 . Mister Rogers' Neighborhood. Series Summary. PBS.org. http://www.pbs.org/parents/rogers/series/summary.html (accessed: July 20, 2015).

19 . stress. Dictionary.com. Dictionary.com Unabridged. Random House, Inc. http://dictionary.reference.com/browse/stress (accessed: July 20, 2015).

20 . Wikipedia contributors, "Walter Bradford Cannon," Wikipedia, The Free Encyclopedia, https://en.wikipedia.org/w/index.php?title=Walter_Bradford_Cannon&oldid=666213690 (accessed August 17, 2015).

21 . Wikipedia contributors, "Fight-or-flight response," Wikipedia, The Free Encyclopedia, https://en.wikipedia.org/w/index.php?title=Fight-or-flight_response&oldid=670660031 (accessed August 17, 2015).

22 . Levine, Peter A. 1997. Waking the tiger: healing trauma : the innate capacity to transform overwhelming experiences. Berkeley, Calif: North Atlantic Books.

23 . Chubbuck, Paul. "Fight, Flight, Freeze." Releasing The Past. November 13, 2010. http://www.releasingthepast.com/fight-flight-freeze/. (accessed October 1, 2015).

Chapter 6
The EMOTIONS Piece

24. Lao Tzu. "Lao Tzu Quotes". GoodReads.com. http://www.goodreads.com/author/show/2622245.Lao_Tzu (accessed: July 22, 2015).

25 . Meyer, Dr. Cindy. Emotions Versus Feelings. http://emotionaldetective.typepad.com/emotional-detective/2012/04/emotions-vs-feelings.html (accessed: September 1, 2015).

Chapter 7
The CONFRONTATION Piece

26. Dale Partridge. "Dale Partridge Quotes". GoodReads.com. http://www.goodreads.com/author/show/8145659.Dale_Partridge (accessed: July 22, 2015).

Chapter 8
The READY Piece

27. Walt Disney. "Walt Disney Quotes". GoodReads.com. http://www.goodreads.com/author/show/3510823.Walt_Disney_Company (accessed: July 22, 2015).

Conclusion

28. Ernest Hemingway. "Ernest Hemingway Quotes". GoodReads.com. http://www.goodreads.com/author/show/1455.Ernest_Hemingway (accessed: July 29, 2015).

Meet The Author

CALVIN WITCHER is a sought after thought-leader, conference speaker, and workshop facilitator in the fields of philosophy, spirituality, and personal development. Through his websites, books, workshops, and other mediums, Calvin teaches others how to discover their highest potential in every transition of life.

Life began with Calvin growing up in a single family home in what many called, "the projects"; a community often associated with poverty, drugs and violence. Wanting something different, he turned to spirituality where he learned principles that drastically changed his life for the better. He now thrives on teaching people how to create what they want even with the broken pieces of their life.

Calvin actively mentors and trains thousands in family education, spirituality and personal development across the nation. He has been in high demand since 1998 and is a recognized expert within the professional, academic, spiritual and parenting communities.

Calvin currently resides in Los Angeles with his husband, Jeremy and their four sons, Daniel, Kendrick, Brian and Dante along with their dog, London.

Calvin Witcher is available for speaking, teaching, consulting and counseling. For media inquiries, ideas for collaboration and more information, please visit CalvinWitcher.com

www.ingramcontent.com/pod-product-compliance
Lightning Source LLC
Chambersburg PA
CBHW021227090426
42740CB00006B/422